APPRECIATION

I would like to thank my sister, Rita for inspiring me to write this book. Her continued belief in my ability to write a book, and her inspirational visions shared with me, was an epiphany to my prayer request for direction for my calling to help God's people. She has seen me through some of the most challenging times in my life, and continues to support me on my personal journey from grief to strength.

From GRIEF to STRENGTH

A MESSAGE OF HOPE TO HELP FIND STRENGTH TO MOVE ON WHEN YOUR WORLD HAS BEEN TURNED UPSIDE DOWN:

DEVASTATING LOSS,
MAJOR SET BACK,
SICKNESS,
DISEASE,
TRAGEDY,
COVID-19

NITA REEVON

WESTBOW
PRESS®
A DIVISION OF THOMAS NELSON
& ZONDERVAN

WestBow Press books may be ordered through booksellers or by contacting:

WestBow Press
A Division of Thomas Nelson & Zondervan
1663 Liberty Drive
Bloomington, IN 47403
www.westbowpress.com
844-714-3454

Unless otherwise noted, scripture taken from the King James Version of the Bible.

Scripture quotations marked (CEV) are from the Contemporary English Version Copyright © 1991, 1992, 1995 by American Bible Society. Used by Permission.

ISBN: 978-1-6642-4799-4 (sc)
ISBN: 978-1-6642-4800-7 (hc)
ISBN: 978-1-6642-4798-7 (e)

Library of Congress Control Number: 2021921708

Print information available on the last page.

WestBow Press rev. date: 12/06/2021

CONTENTS

INTRODUCTION

Heavenly Father, I thank you for the opportunity to minister to my readers through the life experiences shared in this book, "From Grief to Strength".

I pray that everyone who read or hear these words, see that there is hope from whatever illusion that has led them to believe that there is no hope. I asked for wisdom to share with anyone going through grief and pain during this pandemic time. My prayer is that everyone will be able to grieve loses they are experiencing, have experienced or may experience in the future, and return to a state of power and strength. I pray that healing is received through the victorious outcomes from the stories in this book. I also pray that your own stories will be shared to help someone else to heal from whatever they may be going through as well.

THE COMFORT OF THE HOLY SPIRIT

Lord, I am an emotional creature. I was created to experience emotions. I feel deeply. I rejoice and laugh. I also hurt and cry. It's just part of being human. It's who I am. At times, I mourn. I weep in deep grief over someone or something lost. I experience grief when I lose a loved one. I feel it when I lose a long-held dream. When something that means so much is taken from me, it is natural that I would grieve. Lord, please comfort me in such times.

"Blessed are they that mourn: for they shall be comforted"
Matthew 5:4

1

GRIEF

THERE ARE MILLIONS of books and topics written every day on grief, pain and suffering, because the world is full of people that are hurting. We have seen tragedies happening all over the world for as far back as we can remember. When we turn on the television news, we hear of tragedies happening every day. Before we can unlock our cell phones, we see news flashes of murders, tragedies, deadly shootings, accidents, tornados, hurricanes, earthquakes, bombings, abductions, rapes, home invasions, robberies, starvation, animal abuse, economic disasters, police brutalities, political scandals, wars or rumors of wars around the world. Oh, now let's not forget what is dominating the airways today, The Coronavirus Pandemic – COVID-19.

We have seen devastating earthquakes, tornados and hurricanes that displaced millions of people. Some of us may have volunteered our services to render help or may have sent relief through donations of food, resources, and/or money. Others may have watched in unbelief and thanked God it was on the other side of the world, and not on their street.

If the world has never known grief, we know it now. By now, we all have known or heard of someone who has suffered the loss of a loved one during this pandemic plague. Some of the stories have been utterly horrific that it's depressing to have to listen about it on the news.

What if the news report was about you or someone you hold dear to your heart? There is no turning the channel or turning off the television. You are actually living the reality of the nightmare, the tragedy, the grief, the pain, and the suffering. Oh, but when it hits your front door. What do you do? How do you respond? Where do you start picking up the pieces of fragments of your life when grief or tragedy strikes your front door? Many of us do not recognize the pain and suffering of others until it is at our own front door.

What is Grief?

Grief is a natural response to loss. It's the emotional- psychological experience you feel when something or someone you love is lost. The pain of loss can feel overwhelming. It follows a loss of any kind, such as a relationship, a status, a job, a house, a friendship, a miscarriage, a health illness, a pet, or income. When there is a loss caused by the death of someone we love, the grief may be more intense.

> **The goal is to be able to come to terms with your loss, find new meaning, and eventually move on with your life.**

You may experience a rainbow of emotions, from shock or anger to disbelief, guilt, and profound sadness. The pain of grief can impact your physical and mental health, causing insomnia, loss of appetite, depression, diminished interpersonal relationships, or unusual behaviors. These are normal reactions to loss.

One of life's biggest challenges is coping with the loss of someone or something you love. Whatever the cause of your grief, there are healthy ways to cope with the pain, in time, and ease your sadness. The goal is to be able to come to terms with your loss, find new meaning and eventually move on with your life.

A lot of times, those around us, do not acknowledge other forms of grief outside of death. Whatever the significant loss to you, remember you have a right to grieve. Your pain may be compounded by the feelings that no one has given you "permission" to experience grief. That's when you need to know that someone cares and will respond with compassion.

"The Lord is nigh unto them that are of a broken heart; and saveth such as be of a contrite spirit". **Psalm 34:18**

Some people never recover from their loss. They suffer major depression, psychological and psychosocial disorders. Many turn to drugs and/or alcohol, exhibit aberrant behavior, they lose their mind, or they die of grief. The hospitals, clinics, prisons, and streets are full of people who have lost their way. It's very sad to sit back and witness someone we love struggling to deal with grief. It is as equally sorrowful to experience grief yourself while attempting to support your grieving loved one.

How do you support someone else during their grieving if you are grieving yourself? It depends on the individual grieving. You must first acknowledge your own feelings. Sometimes it helps to help someone else when you are going through a difficult time yourself. We must allow everyone to grieve in their own way. No two people will grieve the same. One grieving person may want space. If so, we must respect their decision to have their space. Others may want the closeness of hugs, kisses, holding of hands or just need someone to listen to how they are feeling. Do not force your opinions on others. Allow them to grieve at their own pace.

It may be more overwhelming to have to respond to some of the things that people want to say, in an attempt to be comforting. Don't push. Simply listen in silence as you share your own empathetic presence.

One can offer to walk with them through whatever they are going through. Some may need words of encouragement or simply a confirmation of knowing that if they need something that you can do for them, they can count on you to be there and come through for them.

> **We go through pain and suffering, to help others coming after us.**

Many people do find the strength they need to go on, to overcome the grief and are able to move into a position of strength and empowerment. You have to find a reason to go on. You must focus on the good and not the loss. Anything that we give our attention to the most, grows the fastest in our lives. That is why we hear people tell us all the time to think positive thoughts.

What were the good things that you enjoyed most about the person, the job, or the thing that you lost? When you think about why you are grieving, you are missing the things that brought you joy, happiness or made you laugh, smile or even cry at times. We must have a spirit of gratitude for even the littlest things in remembering our precious relational experiences that will no longer exist. We must find other fulfilling things to do. Some people do things in memory of the person or situation that no longer exist.

My prayer for you is that you will be comforted and strengthened during your loss experience, and be able to return to a state of power and strength. I have selected a few stories of hope and triumph that I pray you can glean some insight from. As you read the stories, let them help shed a positive light on your situation and minister to your spirit.

We all go through life experiences, but the pain we experience is not for ourselves. We go through pain and suffering to help others coming after us. Once we have made it to the other side of the pain and suffering, we should reach back and help those who have lost all hope so they too can come through stronger on the other side of the pain and grief.

The Stages of Grief and the Processes of Grief

You cannot write a book on grief without mentioning the stages of grief and the processes of grief. So, let's cover the formalities and basic understanding of some of the grief processes. It is a tool that has been used as a guide for years by therapists and counselors. The Psychiatrist Elisabeth Kubler-Ross wrote in her 1969 book *"On Death & Dying"*, that people should expect to experience only 5 Stages: denial, anger, bargaining, depression, and acceptance in that order. I was introduced to this model during nursing school over 30 years ago. However, it is not true, because people are unpredictable and have highly individualized grieving.

Stage models have been adjusted to reflect what therapists and counselors are seeing with individuals. These stages are a general guide of what to expect, because stages can hit at the same time, or occur out of order.

The 7 Stages of Grief

SHOCK AND DENIAL	The reactions of learning of the loss may be numbness or disbelief.
PAIN AND GUILT	The actions of trying to escape the pain with drugs and/or alcohol, bad habits or may feel remorse.
ANGER AND BARGAINING	Statements made such as "I will never drink again if you just bring him/her back".
DEPRESSION, REFLECTION, LONELINESS	May realize the true magnitude of your loss and it is depressing; may feel empty
THE UPWARD TURN	May start to feel better.
RECONSTRUCTION AND WORKING THROUGH	Reconstruct yourself without your loved one – consider new life activities.
ACCEPTANCE AND HOPE	Deal with the reality of your situation and start planning for your future – find joy again.

How do you deal with grief?

Well, you might ask, how do I do that? You must first acknowledge your pain. You hear people say, I'm ok, I'm fine, or I'm not hurting. Admit that you are hurting and in pain. Once you acknowledge your pain, you can then be open to healing. Understand that grief can trigger many different and unexpected emotions. Once you know that feelings of grief may be triggered by the most unexpected event, you don't have to explain your emotions. It's ok to grieve whenever it hits. Your grieving process is unique to you.

You may choose to seek out support from people who care about you, talk to a therapist or grief counselor, or draw support from a clergy member from a religious community. During this time, this may best be done through video chats or phone calls, if there is no one available to speak with you at home. You can find support groups that do online groups or conference calls. Talking with people with similar experiences of loss will help you much more than someone who has never experienced your loss. Don't be afraid to reach out. Don't isolate yourself even more than the impact from the COVID-19 restrictions. It's never too late to meet and build new relationships.

You must support yourself emotionally by taking care of yourself physically, mentally, and spiritually. You must eat even when you do not feel like eating. You must drink plenty of fluids unless contraindicated medically. Hydration is vital to our health. Move around and you will feel better. If you can, take a walk or simply move your upper body. When you lay around lifeless, life is drained from your body. This can lead to depression which can sometimes be hard to distinguish from grief.

If you cannot move physically, then move mentally. See yourself in your mind moving, walking, or dancing. This process can be accomplished through one of my favorite things to do, which is meditation. When we meditate, we focus our attention on a single object, internal or external. It is a mental practice exercise that involves relaxation, focus, and awareness. Meditation is to the mind what physical exercise is to the body. The practice is usually done in a still seated position, and with your eyes closed.

Spiritually we can pray about whatever is on your mind. This may be difficult if you have never prayed. I have met lots of people on my journey who have never prayed or dealt with anyone on any spiritual level. If you are grieving, you can reach out to someone in your spiritual community to pray for you, you can watch Christian Television broadcasts, or you can say a simple prayer privately for yourself, expressing your emotions in prayer asking for guidance for the next step or for the pain to be lifted.

You can memorialize your loved one in your daily life by remembering the things that made you laugh or smile. Wearing a piece of jewelry in remembrance of them, making a memorial pillow out of a favorite garment of theirs, create a scrapbook or wall of photos, or eating one of their favorite dishes. Some people make a memorial page on social media to share with others during this social distance time. It's a way to reach out and help others share in your loved one's remembrance. You can also make visits to the burial site on special holidays or set times. You can incorporate memorializing your loved one in a way that was specific and unique to them. When you focus on the positive things that mattered the most, it will help you to deal with the grief. If no one is around, we must encourage ourselves. Social media has become popular ways to express what you are thinking or feeling, or it may be used to inform a wide audience of a loved one's passing to reach out for support. Reading messages from people can be a source of encouragement and often provide comfort for you during the grieving of your loss.

You can say this short simple prayer:

"Loving Father, I thank you for strengthening me as I am dealing with this loss. I pray you keep your loving arms of protection around me and help me to overcome this pain and grief. I am hurting and sad, but you have promised to never leave me or forsake me. Thank you for comforting me".

Amen

Salvation Prayer

If you don't have a relationship with our Heavenly Father, but you are willing to have a relationship with Him, you can pray this simple prayer:

"Lord, I confess my sins and ask for your forgiveness. I ask you to come into my heart as my Lord and Savior. I receive Your Holy Spirit as my Comforter to help me to obey You and to do Your will. I thank you for saving me in Jesus Name". Amen

According to Romans 10:9-10, it says "That if thou shalt confess with thy mouth the Lord Jesus, and shalt believe in thine heart that God hath raised him from the dead, thou shalt be saved. For with the heart man believeth unto righteousness; and with the mouth confession is made unto salvation".

You are saved by simply confessing that you are a sinner, asking for forgiveness, welcoming Jesus into your heart as your Lord and Savior, and believing that He died for you and was raised from the dead. It is a simple 2 step process. You say with your mouth...then you believe in your heart. If you are having difficulty believing, pray for help for your unbelief.

Keep a journal and write down your feelings. Document what you pray about and expect an answer.

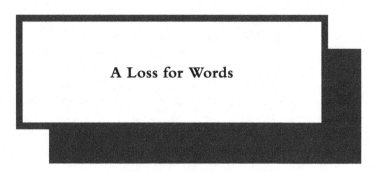

A Loss for Words

Sometimes people do not know what to say to someone who has lost a loved one, or something dear to them. It can be awkward trying to comfort someone. I know people who totally avoid you, because they don't know what to say. If you are at a loss for word, you can simply say:

(1)   I am sorry for your loss

(2)   I wish I had the right words to say to you

(3)   A simple hug without words can speak volumes

(4)   "We all need somebody to lean on when we are not strong" just tell them you are just a phone call away

(5)   Tell them you will keep them in your prayers

(6)   Offer them a short on-the-spot comforting prayer if they are open to it

2

◦◦◦

LETTING GO AND FORGIVENESS

When it's Hard to Let Go of Someone You Love

SOMETIMES WHEN YOU have not personally experienced a significant loss, you may not understand what the grieving person is experiencing. You may feel that it should be time for that person to "get over it" and move on with life.

If that grieving person desires to be alone with their sad reflections, please allow them their space. It is a normal reaction. Having some knowledge of the stages of grief and the processes can be helpful to the griever and the comforter. This enables the griever to deal with those seemingly, inconsiderate outside pressures of those wanting to expedite the grieving process. Remember, you are acting normal. They just don't get it.

There is no specific time frame for feelings of pain after we experience a loss. Some may say "more" grief is better or that there is a proper way to grieve. Those ridiculous statements can make the process more difficult. For some people, grief can be short. They may feel pain initially, and seem to get over it, but the pain may return unexpectedly, at the oddest time. Others may experience a prolonged grief that may last months or even years.

It is inevitable that pain and grief will find you if you continue to live in this life. However, without help and support, such pain and grief can lead to isolation, chronic loneliness, and more severe illnesses. We all feel sorrow, sadness and grieve of a loss at some point in our lives. We must learn to express our feelings, cope with our losses, and find the strength to move on especially when it is a death of a loved one.

In Psalm 6:6, David cries out, "I am weary with my groaning; all the night make I my bed to swim; I water my couch with my tears." This Psalmist was crying out in prayer. He was letting God know that he was hurting and was exhausted from the constant sadness he was experiencing. He let Him know how he was feeling. This is exactly what He wants you to do. Cry out to Him and tell Him how you are feeling. Be brutally honest and express your anger, your fears, and any other emotion that you may be feeling. He already knows our pain, struggles and disappointments. He is waiting for you to open your mouth and invite him in to comfort you. He will embrace your honesty and comfort you.

Support groups can be a great resource for comfort. Listening to stories of others who are going through what you are experiencing, helps you to know that you are not alone. People can overcome even the most painful life situations when you know that you are not the only one experiencing a devastating life event. Also, when you share your feelings in a support group, you help others to heal from their losses as well. With support, you can heal and regain the ability to function and move forward in your life.

If you are struggling with religion or participating in support groups, reach out and seek some type of counseling. It is important that you get the help that you need, because you are incredibly resilient and will get through this difficult time in your life. You must take care of you by any means necessary. You have everything you need inside of you, far more than you could ever imagine. Sometimes it takes talking about it with a professional to help you see the good that is left in your life.

Cultural bias can affect or influence how much support someone may get when asked to seek counseling. There may be cultural stigma that may make it harder for some people to talk openly about their feelings or ask for help. Some Cultures view seeking help for mental health treatment as a sign of weakness. This can further isolate you and make your situation seem unbearably hopeless. Our mental health is as equally important as our physical health.

We Must Forgive and Let Go of Anger

"A More Excellent Way", by Dr. Henry W. Wright is one of my favorite books on discovering spiritual pathways to health. It is a great resource to help understand the spiritual aspects behind many diseases of the spirit, body and soul. He reminds us that we have a personal responsibility to take control of our health. He elaborates on identifying root causes to specific diseases and offer pathways of healing and wholeness.

A common root cause that precipitates a lot of our sicknesses and diseases are caused by our own unwillingness to forgive or let go. When we hold onto painful things, we are only hurting ourselves. We must forgive and let go. Forgiveness is a process that starts with being willing to forgive, then making the decision to forgive. It may be difficult for you in the beginning, depending on the situation in which you must forgive. Be honest about your feelings and gradually let go.

Forgiveness is a gift you give to yourself by releasing the resentments and freeing yourself. If we are angry due to our loss, we must start to focus on the present; the here and now. We must replace the anger and bitterness with joy, peace and happiness by picking up the pieces and moving on with life.

When it's Hard to Forgive

There are millions of cases where loved ones have been lost due to careless, reckless behaviors of others, such as school and church shootings, plane crashes, medical malpractices, house fires, drownings, national disasters, and many other incidents where someone else caused the loss of someone significant to us. According to the Centers for Disease Control and Prevention (CDC), in December 2020, COVID-19 became the third leading cause of death for people between ages of 45 and 84 following heart disease and cancer. People under age 35, drug overdoses, suicide, and car crashes remained the leading cause of death in the United States. Kidney disease was high on the list as well. I added kidney disease to the list of causes of death, because I had to forgive myself for causing damage to my own kidneys a few years ago. I was taking over-the-counter Motrin for back pain every night and found myself one stage from requiring Kidney Dialysis. I was very disappointed with the news, but I chose to believe for my healing. Kidney failure is not reversible. It can only be slowed down from progressing to the next stage. Fortunately for me, my kidney damaged was reversed.

When a death occurs resulting from a car accident, family members are often left grief-stricken, and angry. They are often shocked and in denial. The anger is usually directed at the culprit responsible for the fatal car accident. It was totally unexpected with no chance to say goodbye, resulting in grievous, emotional pain.

Sheena was only 14 years old when she was tragically killed in a car accident. While hanging out with a group of teenagers, joy riding in a local state park, a teen-aged driver lost control of the car, and crashed into a tree. It was reported that the teens were taking turns driving, in which none had a driver's license. The peer pressure from the teens encouraged the driver to go faster, exceeding the speed limit. Suddenly, there was a sharp turn, causing him to lose control. As he slammed on the brakes, it was too late. The vehicle he was driving slid off the road and slammed into a tree hitting the side where Sheena had been sitting.

When the driver attempted to open the doors to help the other passengers out, he saw Sheena trapped between the airbag and the dashboard. She was bleeding profusely with a severe head injury that was incompatible with life. She died on impact. It took the Jaws of Life to open the door and pull her from the totally wrecked vehicle. The driver emerged from the vehicle with nothing more than a few scratches. Non-the-less, he says it's an image that still haunts him to this day.

The mother was devastated. She lost her only daughter to a senseless, reckless accident. When everyone heard about what happened to her it was overwhelming tragic news. The mother having to identify the body and live with the mental image of that reality for the rest of her life, took this tragedy to an entirely different level. She will tell you that not a day goes by that she does not think of her little girl. She had to be strong for her other children and go on with her life. She knows she must forgive. Nevertheless, she is still struggling to forgive the driver. She is angry that her daughter was not afforded the opportunity to enjoy a full adult life, because it was taken at such a young age. She wanted the driver to pay for the mistake that he made. He was convicted of negligent homicide and placed on intensive probation prohibiting him from obtaining a driver's license until he was nearly done with his college career. They were all very young children who made poor choices to get into the vehicle for a joyride that turned tragic. It was an accident. It could have been any of those children or the driver to die that day.

There were some additional penalties and charges against him in a civil lawsuit. Although, he says he intends to eventually pay the civil judgement charges against him, the penalty has not yet been paid. I am sure that his procrastination to pay the judgement, adds to her inability to forgive him. It appears to her that he has gone on with his life and left her life in shambles to pick up the pieces.

The driver chose not to self-destruct or hold grudges against those people who called him a murderer and made threats against his life. He made a mistake that cost someone their life which could have possibly cost him his life and future as well. He chose to rise above the circumstances and deal with the consequences of his actions. He pressed on in a positive direction and continues to live a productive life. I am sure he will have even greater success once he makes the financial amends with the still grieving family. Perhaps he may have had his own reasons for not paying the restitution ordered by the court. Regardless of the personal reasons for not complying with the court order, his failure to comply adds to the pain and suffering of the victim's family.

We must discoverer how to let go of resentment and overcome the resistance to forgive. Sometimes people are just not willing to make things right. Even if they never apologize, we must do our part to free ourselves from the pain and suffering.

This mother has a choice also. She can release the driver from the debt and forgive him. It has been many years since the tragic accident. She appears to have moved on and is actively involved in caring for her extended family, and her own personal health issues. When you see her, you would never know that she went through such a tragic death of her only daughter. She is always smiling, and cheerful on the surface, but deep down inside, she holds the bitterness in her heart. It comes out from time to time, but she refuses to let go and totally forgive. She has suffered additional personal and family tragedies. I strongly believe that whenever she chooses to forgive the driver, who crashed the van, I believe she will see physical and mental healing beyond her wildest imagination. I truly believe her physical illnesses that keep re-occurring is in direct relationship to her anger and bitterness, she holds in her heart towards the driver.

She looks to fill the void with involvement with positive activities and making every effort to focus on the good times. I commend her ability to still stand strong in the face of the multiple tragedies she has experienced in her life. The law of attraction is in full force here. Positive thoughts attract positive events. Negative thoughts attract negative events. She keeps attracting more tragedy, by not releasing the bitter, angry images embedded in her memory.

The bible clearly tells us in several different scriptures throughout the bible, that we must forgive others as we have need of forgiveness ourselves.

Psychologists define forgiveness as a conscious, deliberate decision to release feelings of resentment or vengeance toward a person or group who has hurt you. It does not mean that you forget what has happened or continue to have them in your life. You let go for yourself. The anger and bitterness held inside of you only destroys and hurt you further. It does nothing for the culprit who inflicted the pain. In an effort to have a broken heart healed, we must be willing to let go of the anger and forgive.

You can express your hurt and honest feelings through prayer by simply praying about what you are feeling. Verbally release the person who hurt you or caused you pain and grief. This verbal relief goes both ways. If you are the one responsible for causing the pain and/or grief, you too can release it as well. If you can speak directly to the person, tell them that you forgive them or write them a letter. When we truly release someone through forgiveness, the heaviness of the burden is lifted. A shift occurs in the atmosphere and healing is released. This works for people who are still alive and for those who have passed on. If you are unable to speak directly with the person, some people have found it helpful to write it out on a piece of paper and burn it once the commitment has been made in your heart to let it go. The burning signifies total release, when you truly believe in your heart that you have forgiven the person or situation that you held a grudge against.

Never allow un-forgiveness to block any of your blessings. The Human Spirit is amazing; it is remarkable and resilient. It has a way of healing even the worse of injuries mentally, physically, and spiritually.

3

HEALING

Sometimes People Do Get Healed

WE HEAR OF testimonies of people being healed from cancers, brain injuries, recovering from tragic accidents and various other medical diagnoses and illnesses. We see ministers praying for the sick and people being healed at church services. Believers pray for one another and sometimes see that individual helped, who may have been suffering from a devastating illness. Usually when we see healing, we first see a believer with a high level of faith joining their faith with other believers operating in their spiritual gifts. Healing can occur with a willing recipient and some powerful believers that it can and will be done.

You can believe for healing for yourself as well. Once you make up your mind that you shall be healed and begin to see yourself healed, no force will be able to keep you from receiving your healing. Every circumstance that tries to stand in your way will have to bow its knee to your command and release your healing. It takes a deep personal revelation of your inner strength for healing power, to stand strong in faith without wavering, regardless of what circumstances or symptoms come against you.

However, if the individual cannot exercise authority for themselves over the, diseases, and unwanted circumstances, we may need intercessors to intercede on their behalf. An Intercessor is one who fights or pleads for justice, to petition on behalf of another. An Intercessor prays on behalf of another to find favor for whatever the other person stands in need of.

Matthew 18:20, for **where two or three are gathered together**, in **my name**, there am I, in the midst of them.

If My Dog Can Receive Healing, So Can You

The world is full of animal lovers who love their pets and consider them a significant part of the family. I have had several pets over the years. I had one pet that I truly loved dearly. He ran out of the house one night and took off down the street. He was missing. I couldn't find him. Sometime during the night, he was hit by a car. I posted flyers throughout the neighborhood the very next morning, offering a reward for my dog to be returned to me. The person who found him, called me and told me that he had taken him to the emergency Veterinarian Hospital. I contacted the hospital and went to claim my little dog. When I arrived, I was told that his back had been broken and he was paralyzed. The Veterinarian told me he would never walk again. He further added that he recommended that I just put him to sleep. I refused to listen to his findings. I asked if there was anything else that could be done. He told me that an X-ray would not determine if his spine was severed or if the paralysis was being caused by excessive swelling of his spine. He said he would have to perform surgery to assess his spinal cord. I requested that he do everything possible to give him the best possible chance of survival. My decision would be based on the findings of the condition of his spinal cord. If it was severed, I would put him to sleep, but if it was not, I was going to keep the faith for his healing. The doctor replied it was still a 99.9 % chance that my dog would be still be paralyzed even after the surgery. He did not say 100%, so I chose to stand on the 0.1% chance and believe my dog would be healed.

Of course, everyone thought I had lost my mind and told me to just have him put to sleep and move on. I was grieving and not willing to just let him go without a fight. I loved my pet and paid the $3000.00 to have the surgery and to purchase the Caine-Cart used in his recovery. The cart was used to allow him mobility to still go for walks and have mobility during his paralysis. I posted my scripture on the refrigerator door concerning healing and blocked out all negative voices who tried to discourage me from believing for his healing. I performed physical therapy exercising his little legs four times a day, speaking life to those paralyzed limbs. He wore little pampers, but he was smiling again and eager to go for walks daily. His little spirit was lifted, knowing that I loved him. One day during the exercises, I noticed that he was kicking his little legs on his own. I was so excited and so was he. The feeling in his limbs had returned and he was able to walk again after four months of prayer, faith, and therapy. I truly believed that he would be healed and he was.

Why Sit Here and Die?

During that same time while my dog was recovering from his paralysis, I was assigned to care for a 40-year-old policeman who had been paralyzed from his neck down. He had been shot in his back during a routine traffic stop. He could only turn his head from side to side. This officer was very angry and bitter. He cursed all the nursing staff daily and refused anyone to care for him. His behavior was so bad, that the Administrator called for an outside Private Duty Nursing Agency for nurses to come into the facility to care for him. He had burned out an entire staff of nurses in a nearly 600 bed hospital. He had pushed away all family and friends to include every nurse who had been assigned to care for him. He was depressed and told me that he just wanted to be left alone and wanted to die.

I was one of the private duty nurses called in to care for him. Immediately, he told me to get out of his room and leave him alone. He gave me the same rude, disrespectful belligerent words that he had been giving to the staff for the past eight months. I introduced myself to him and told him that it did not matter how bad he spoke to me, because I was not going anywhere. I had been assigned to work with him 7 days a week for 12 hours each day. I asked if he would allow me to assess his wound to his back, because I could smell that it was rotten. He told me "NO". I sat the first day out. I prayed for guidance on how to handle him.

The next day when I reported to work, I re-introduced myself to him and told him that I wanted to share a testimony with him. I told him about my little dog who had been hit by a car and was paralyzed. I told him that he had healed after four months and my dog was walking again. I shared with him the therapy I did for him daily and how I had believed for his healing.

I remember telling him, "If my dog can be healed, imagine how much more you are worth than a dog"? He looked up at me with tears in his eyes. I asked him if I could pray for him to be healed too. He said "Yes". We both cried, then I explained that I needed his cooperation. He allowed me to help get his infection under control by changing his wound dressings. His entire back and buttocks had deep holes from laying in the same spot without moving for months. That was the beginning. He began to look forward to my shifts. He had a glimpse of hope. He began to also let the physical therapists, occupational therapist and other disciplines do their jobs as well.

The seasons had changed. He allowed me to take him outside to sit in the sunshine, in a Geri Chair for the first time in over eight months. The number 8 in Biblical numerology, means new beginning; it denotes "a new order or creation. When the Administration saw him outside smiling, looking good and smelling good, they made a huge celebration of the occasion. His movement to his upper extremities gradually returned which gave him more incentive to continue with therapy. His wounds began to heal, and he was eating again. He was beginning to receive his healing. His progress improved tremendously, and he was later transferred to an acute rehab center where they had reported he was making significant progress. Once he began to witness his own progress, he had hope. He began to believe that he too could be healed and began to imagine himself whole again. His mental image of his body had changed which was causing the physical changes on the outside. The Mind is a very powerful thing. His will to live, overruled his determination to die. My mission there was done.

I went on to share the story of my little dogs' healing with many paralyzed patients over the years. Those who were ready to move on, and believe that they too could be healed, experienced significant progress back to a state of independence. Some changed their perspective outlook for their future and found positive ways to reach back and help others, even when they did not receive full recovery of the use of their limbs. I believe we can always find some good in every situation if we seek it diligently. I am sure that there are so many more success stories out there of people recovering from tragedies.

That police officer was shot in the line of duty, as with so many other officers. Police officers take an oath to protect the citizens and respect the Constitution of the United States even with capturing the "Bad Guys". It is a tragedy to see innocent officers get injured or killed in the line of duty. Their families and friends are grieved by their loss and must find a way to go on as well.

It is equally sad for the families of the victims who have suffered in the past and recently, serious injuries and violent deaths from the hands of police officers who have inflicted the use of excessive force in apprehending suspects. They too, must find a way to grieve and go on with their lives. The victim or their families may have a viable lawsuit against the arresting officers or even the municipalities that employ them, but that can never replace the life of a loved one. When the killings make national news, the pain, grief and suffering is prolonged by having to relive each publicized airing of the murderous events. Although some police officers were charged and sentenced to prison in some of the cases, it can never take the place of the lives destroyed by the over-use of physical law enforcement used to murder the victims. My heart and prayers go out to all of the family and friends of victims who are still grieving the loss of loved ones due to police brutality.

Things that can be done to help the victims deal with their grief and pain range from, participating in peaceful movements against police brutality by organizing "die-in protests", marches, and demonstrations in response to the killings that show support for the family and loved ones of the deceased. Making your voice heard through social media, donating to families to help with funeral and legal needs, and reporting what you have witnessed. Do not be afraid to speak up to help remove bad officers and criminals. Report what you see anonymously to Tip Hotline: 1-800-78-CRIME, if you are afraid to come forth. Send videos of inappropriate behaviors observed, as proof of what really happened. Encourage emotional support and counseling. The families need to know that they are not alone and that there are people who care.

Sadly, the trend of fatal police shootings in the United States seems to only be increasing, with a total 132 civilians having been shot, 16 of whom were Black, in the first two months of 2021. In 2020, there were 1,004 fatal police shootings, and in 2019 there were 999 fatal shootings. Additionally, the rate of fatal police shootings among Black Americans was much higher than that for any other ethnicity, standing at 35 fatal shootings per million of the population as of February 2021 according to an article on statistics from NVDRS. I commend the good officers out there, to include my own family members, who have sworn to serve, protect and uphold the Constitution of the United States.

Romans 12:18, If it be possible, as much as lieth in you, live peaceably with all men.

Healing May Not Come

A friend of mine shared with me the grief and anguish of the loss of her daughter's only son. He had been born with a hole in his heart and suffered from multiple medical problems. He had under-went various surgeries to have his little heart defect repaired. He had tubes in nearly all of his little orifices. His mother loved the child and chose to carry him to term, even when the prognosis of his illness had been diagnosed from the womb. She loved her son and took excellent care of him until he suffered a debilitating pneumonia. He was intubated and placed on a life support machine in the Pediatric Intensive Care Unit at a Children's hospital for approximately two months.

At one point and time, he appeared to be responding to treatment. Unfortunately, he took a turn for the worse. The family had to make a decision whether or not to keep allowing this baby to continue to suffer at the hands of experimental medicine. This is a very difficult, ethical decision that millions of families struggle to make. This family made the decision to take him off life support. They gathered everyone together to say their good-byes. Before they could pull the plug, the baby went into cardiac arrest. The ICU team performed CPR until the father insisted that they stop and just let him go. He had fought a good fight. He was a strong little fella. The family was deeply saddened, but they found solace in knowing that their loved one was not suffering anymore. The love of the family for each other during that critical time, helped them all to put aside their own selfish feelings of not wanting to lose the baby, and chose to let him die of natural causes when his heart stopped beating. They were spared of the decision of having to make the life and death decision of pulling the plug. They were grateful they did not have to make the decision amongst themselves to remove him from life support. That spared them the question of "what if we would have just waited a little while longer?

If you have ever made the choice to remove a loved one from a life support device, it can be overwhelming in the midst of that difficult decision. Taking the breathing tube out of a patient relieves them of the discomfort that may be caused by keeping the tube in. It's normal to feel reluctant or an intense burden if you have to decide to remove life support, in which you believe is the only thing keeping your loved one alive. You may feel guilty, sad, or afraid. Just know that you have no power over death itself. Once the life support machine is off, a patient may stop breathing. However, in some cases, a patient may continue to breathe on their own. You can only try to make the treatment choices your loved one would have made. Your decision to keep your loved one from additional suffering is made from love and compassion. You may ask, did we do the right thing? Did our love prevail?

Those are questions that I have heard so many times from families struggling to make that decision and proceeded to remove their loved one from life support. I watched families pray at the bedside, read books, play music, speak to their loved ones, or just hold their hands. I have witnessed many patients start breathing on their own afterwards. Unfortunately, some never recover.

When I asked my friend how her family dealt with the loss of their beloved baby boy, they said, "We did everything we could do while he was alive, and loved him as much as we possibly could". They were at peace knowing that he was no longer suffering. They prayed about their decision and chose to release him. They were blessed with a beautiful, healthy baby girl less than a year later.

Various Pediatric Research facilities cares for approximately 8,600 children with catastrophic diseases each year. That means there are a lot of families dealing with chronically ill children who need support. Things you can do to support them are: Allow them to share their feelings, be a good listener, don't be afraid to ask how they are doing, allow them to feel sad and scared and do not try to force them to have a positive outlook. Keep the atmosphere peaceful, reassure them that their little one's life matters, or just sit quietly with them and let them know you are there for them. Offer to give them a break to go home to get some rest or get them food to help keep them going. If you can afford it, offer financial support or seek support networks for financial assistance, mental support and counseling. Include the child, if at all possible, to assure them that their illness has nothing to do with something they did or said. Allow the child to express their feelings through drawings, crafts or verbally. Answer their questions truthfully. Offer prayer for the family.

A Biblical Story:
David pleads with God for His baby to live

"And Nathan departed unto his house. And the LORD struck the child that Uriah's wife bare unto David, and it was very sick. David therefore besought God for the child; and David fasted, and went in, and lay all night upon the earth. And the elders of his house arose, *and went* to him, to raise him up from the earth: but he would not, neither did he eat bread with them. And it came to pass on the seventh day that the child died. And the servants of David feared to tell him that the child was dead: for they said, Behold, while the child was yet alive, we spake unto him, and he would not hearken unto our voice: how will he then vex himself, if we tell him that the child is dead? But when David saw that his servants whispered, David perceived that the child was dead: therefore, David said unto his servants, is the child dead? And they said, He is dead. Then David arose from the earth, and washed, and anointed *himself*, and changed his apparel, and came into the house of the LORD, and worshipped: then he came to his own house; and when he required, they set bread before him, and he did eat.

Then said his servants unto him, What thing *is* this that thou hast done? thou didst fast and weep for the child, *while it was* alive; but when the child was dead, thou didst rise and eat bread. And he said, While the child was yet alive, I fasted and wept: for I said, Who can tell *whether* GOD will be gracious to me, that the child may live? But now he is dead, wherefore should I fast? Can I bring him back again? I shall go to him, but he shall not return to me". **2 Samuel 12: 15-23**

Once David saw that the baby was dead, he made the decision to move on with his life. David knew that he would be reunited with the baby someday, but life still had to go on for him. He chose to accept the fact that the baby was gone. The scripture does not elaborate whether or not he experienced other emotional feelings later. It simply stated that he made up his mind not to dwell on the fact that he could not bring the baby back. He had prayed and fasted during the time the baby was alive, hoping for a miracle.

People often pray for their loved ones to be healed. Healing miracles do happen, but we do not always see healing miracles. We wonder why some people receive healing and some people die. It's difficult to understand and may add to our grief and suffering. We see great spiritual leaders around the world with healing ministries yet, people die, despite our best prayers and efforts to intercede on their behalf. In this world, death is inevitable. We can pray and plead, through prayer as David did, but we are still left with the unanswered question, as to why?

"Then we which are alive and remain shall be caught up together with them in the clouds, to meet the Lord in the air: and so shall we ever be with the Lord. Wherefore comfort one another with these words". **1 Thessalonians 4:17-18**

4

COVID-19 THE CORONAVIRUS
EXPOSURE

I WAS RECENTLY reminded me of my own recent loss of my dear mother who was buried on March 11, 2020, right before everyone was shut in place due to COVID-19. The day she was buried, they stopped having funerals with gatherings of more than 9-10 people in attendance. My mother had Stage IV Lung Cancer for four and a half years. Upon receiving the lung cancer diagnosis, she began to call everyone she knew to tell them that she was dying. Friends and family began to call her from everywhere and flooded her living room with wall-to-wall cards and flowers. She had a shrine of encouragement, yet she immediately lost her zeal for life.

The cancer diagnosis was a devastating shock. It was totally unexpected. She had only gone to the doctor for an annual physical. She needed a health clearance to continue participating at the gym for her Zumba Classes. She was never sick. She simply had a spot on her lung that the doctor later confirmed with a biopsy that it was cancer. She became depressed and started to plan her funeral. She was reluctant to be treated with the chemo therapy initially, but she pursued it after contemplating the risks and the benefits. She had a wonderful Hematologist, who was very compassionate, kind and gentle with her. We supported our mom by taking her to all of her appointments and encouraging her to continue to live her best life. We had to remind her to speak life over herself. We had to help her to see how blessed she was in the midst of her terminal diagnosis. She still had stamina, no pain, a loving family, grandchildren, great-grandchildren, church members, club members, and people who still needed her. I recall telling her to *"look at her cancer diagnosis as a pimple on your face. If it is not bothering you, don't bother it. You would have never known you had cancer if you had not gone for a physical check-up. You had no symptoms. So don't stop doing what you love to do, continue to do what you love to do as long as you feel good"*.

Once she had mourned over the new cancer diagnosis, and realized that she did not feel any different, she began to change her priorities. She realized that she was surrounded by the people who gave her life the most meaning. She began to give thanks for the little things she had once taken for granted. Her attitude slowly began to change. She became more grateful and appreciative of everything. I am most grateful for the time that we spent over the last few years, traveling and doing the things that gave her the most fulfillment.

The cancer later metastasized to her brain, complicated by a bad case of dementia during her last few months of life. Our family watched her deteriorate from a healthy, active woman who lovingly served in her church, organized and participated in groups that helped others; to a frail woman totally dependent on the love and care from her children. We did everything we could to care for her and was grateful to have been able to do so. We were fortunate to have one another to support each other, as so many people do not. Although we prayed faithfully for our mom to live, she was ready to go. She chose not to live anymore. She told us that she was ready to go and her work here was done. I sat with her during her last night and watched her drop a few tears. I wiped her eyes, held her hand, and told her that if she was ready to go, not worry about us. I told her we will take care of each other. I laid in the bed with her as she closed her eyes and died. I was grateful to have had that experience that I might have missed, if I did not choose to be by her side. Yet, we grieved her loss.

My Mother, Family and Friends Plagued by the COVID-19 Virus

Prior to mom's departure, someone I knew, became gravely ill and had to be placed in the ICU on a ventilator at another hospital. Her husband had contacted us crying and asking us to pray for his wife. He told us the physicians did not know why this healthy woman had become so sick all of a sudden. She had recently come off a cruise ship. She told us that she had first gotten sick on the cruise ship towards the end of 2019, for the entire seven days she was on board. She said her skin was swollen all over, she had a fever, loss of taste, smell, nausea, low blood pressure and swollen lymph nodes. She was told she had some type of infection. She had heard of the mysterious deaths that had occurred on the cruise ship. She was frightened and sought medical attention once she made it back home. She recalls being short of breath and had excessive swelling all over her body, before her major organs shut down.

She and her husband had visited my sister's home after their cruise. They had come by with their pastor to pray for my sister's home. We now belief my mom and brother-in-law were exposed to the deadly COVID-19 virus that she may have contacted on her cruise ship. My mom and she were hospitalized at the same time, at different hospitals. Fortunately, mom recovered after having chest tubes placed into her lungs and treated with antibiotics. However, our sister was struggling for her life across town at another hospital.

She recently told us that she had almost died twice in the hospital when she stopped breathing and her heart had stopped beating. She had been revived through cardiopulmonary resuscitation. The staff did not expect her to live and had called for everyone to come say their goodbyes. During that time, my brother-in-law became very ill with a severe cold that caused him to be on bedrest for days. He is usually never sick. We were very concerned for him as he laid helpless in his quarantined area on the other side of the house in an effort to protect my mom, his wife and the veterans who resided on the property as well.

That single exposure could have taken down our entire family. We did not know about the Coronavirus until after the first of the year. However, people were being exposed and passing it on during that time. We started hearing more and more about the pandemic as it began to spread across the globe.

We believe that she and my brother-in-law, both took the sickness for their families. One of the ministers prophesied that my brother-in-law was in the right place spiritually. His obedience to the Word and his faithfulness to live a righteous lifestyle, not only impacted his health, but the health of everyone in his household.

When we look back at the situation, we now know that the both of them had been infected with the Coronavirus. The minister prophesied that she too had been in right standing and had covered everybody around her as well.

The doctors at the hospital did not know what was causing her not to be able to breath. You can't fix what you don't know what you're dealing with. The COVID-19 virus continues to remain a mystery to the healthcare professionals. Some people turn around and recover and some do not.

My Sister told us that she recalls laying in the hospital bed on the ventilator unable to speak, but said she could hear everything going on all around her. She was praying and saying that she wanted to live. She said she remember having a very strong will to live and determined to fight to breathe if she wanted to live. She said, "Yes, I want to live".

I recently heard my pastor tell us the very same story about his experience of being infected with the COVID-19 virus. He said he was told by the nurses that he had to breathe if he was going to live. The common factors of having a close spiritual relationship, believing for yourself that you will live and not die, fighting for your life and having true Intercessory Prayer Warriors praying on your behalf, were seen with all of them, to include several other friends and family members who were later diagnosed with the COVID-19 virus.

Some people give up when things get tough. If we are ever going to over-come adversities, we must be determined in our heart, mind and soul, to press on and believe in a power much greater than ourselves. I believe this type of strength comes from exercising our faith regularly, before a crisis hit.

My continued prayers go out to the millions of people still suffering from this virus and to those who have lost loved ones due to the virus. My heart goes out to those family members who have to endure being in the hospitals alone without the love and support of their loved ones by their side. As a nurse caring for the families of those who are unable to see their loved ones, I try to treat each and every one of them that I come in contact with, as if they are my very own loved ones.

Although many of those mentioned were in the acute hospital settings, we Americans, saw the greatest tragedies resulting from COVID-19 in our Long-term care facilities. The statistics report that less than 1% of Americans actually live within long-term care facilities, yet over 40% of COVID-19 deaths occurred there. It took a while to establish protocols and to implement specific care pathways in which symptomatic individuals would be treated as they presented to the emergency rooms around the U.S. The initial symptoms to watch out for were primarily the elderly over age 65 with multiple comorbidities, Shortness of breath, fevers greater than 101.0, coughs, generalized malaise and weakness. The local emergency rooms would screen for a minimum of two symptoms before they would agree to accept the patients to be transferred to their emergency room departments. Many would be screened and sent back to the long-term care facilities, which later spread to other elderly patients with compromised immune systems, and staff who worked closely with them.

The protocol of prohibiting outside visitors, screening of staff for possible exposure to individuals infected with the virus, was initiated, but many people did not comply. It was recommended that the use of hand sanitizing upon entering the facility was performed at the door, taking of temperatures, wearing proper PPD (gloves and masks), and answering a series of questions, be done before entering the facility. People failed to admit that they had attended a super-spreader event, worked in another facility where they had been knowing or unknowingly exposed to individuals with the COVID-19 virus, or exposed to someone with the virus in a different setting.

Many healthcare workers were plagued with the fear of contracting COVID-19, yet pushed aside that fear to take care of those in need of nursing care. More panicked and refused to work with positive COVID-19 patients. Some quit their jobs and sought out other avenues of employment, only to find that COVID-19 is everywhere. Others came to work ill, because they have families of their own to care for and bills that need to be paid. With the inadequate supply of PPE, no testing and inconsistencies of hand hygiene and basic social distancing, the spread continued.

There were people that did not believe that the virus could or would affect them until they themselves got sick, saw others ill from it, or witnessed someone they knew die from the virus. Perhaps a lot of deaths that were classified under the "COVID-19" death toll, could have been related to other underlining diseases, nevertheless, it helped raise the number into the thousands for people diagnosed with COVID-19. Regardless of the reason, the fact remains that a lot of lives were lost from the outbreak and the losses continue.

The lockdown tremendously affected the patients and their families over this past year or so, by not being able to see each other. A lot of lives were also lost due to the decline in the health of those who failed to thrive, with notable decrease in their will to live, and from missing their loved ones. The social isolation within the facility kept many confined to their rooms and distant from even those sharing the same room. No one was allowed to go outside or on leave of absences from the facility. A few people took their family members home, but those who could not care for their loved ones at home, had to leave them. The number of deaths were devastating to us all. We continue to grieve throughout this ruinous pandemic as more and more people are being exposed to the pandemic plague, to include the healthcare workers providing the direct care.

The hardest part of this pandemic, is not just losing our loved ones, but having to leave them to die alone. Some mentioned that not being able to have the type of funeral that would normally be provided for them added to the stress. Many churches continue to remain closed and funeral homes are limited to no more than 10-20 people in attendance. Not having any real cure in sight, adds to the stress of whether the emergency vaccines being authorized to be administered, can actually prevent one from getting the virus. A number of cases have been identified where those who have actually taken the vaccines, still contracted COVID-19 and some have actually died as well. The fear continues.

> **The world has changed drastically and will never be the same again.**

COVID-19 Impact

Millions of people all over the world are hurting in various areas of their lives ranging from normal day to day events, such as physical, mental, spiritual, and financial problems. Now we have the added stressors from the Coronavirus Pandemic to deal with. The Virus has caused millions of families to lose their loved ones unexpectedly. To add to the agony, we cannot be at the bedside to support our loved ones and they have to suffer and die alone. Once they die, we can't even gather to celebrate their lives as we once did with a funeral and family/friends gathering.

In my 30 years of nursing ministry, I have been an advocate for those who needed someone to speak on their behalf. I have prayed for those who wanted to receive their eternal salvation before they died. I have held the hands of so many patients who took their last breath. I have witnessed my share of sickness, sadness and grief. I've been in the Emergency Room when families have rushed their loved ones in during a crisis, only to find the halls full of gurneys and not enough staff to attend to the person needing a Code Team to resuscitate them. I remember the doctor looking at me and all of the viable people in need of emergency care, and him choosing not to initiate Advanced Cardiac Life Support (ACLS) protocol. He simply closed the curtain and told the family that there was nothing we could do. The next sound I heard was the shrilling screaming cry of the family. They were grieving uncontrollably right at the bedside in the emergency room. We had time for a few minutes of consolation, then it was back to work for the next person requiring medical attention.

That incident happened during a time that we did not have a pandemic crisis. Today, there is no consultation room to assist grieving families and friends. Nobody is allowed in the hospital, but the patient. So, imagine what the emergency rooms and ICU's are dealing with today. We are hearing about the massive number of patients requiring critical care support, needing ventilators and staff qualified to care for these patients. The hospitals may be forced to do emergency crash course trainings for ancillary staff to be able to help keep up with the massive number of patients coming into the hospital. The house-keepers and dietary workers may become frontline healthcare workers in a critical situation. It may be happening in some communities already.

I guess we should be grateful for all hands-on deck. Sometimes it is almost easier to handle an influx of patients when we do not have the families monitoring our every move. No offensive to families, it's just that care can be interrupted when we have to stop to care for the families, in addition to the patient, as a lot of families can be very demanding. It takes time to properly dress and undress in our protective gear, (gowns, gloves, masks) in some instances, hoods, booties, face shields and goggles), just to see the next patient... It is very time consuming. Everyone is task oriented and stretched to the max.

I know for a fact that I would have been heart-broken if I could not have been at the bedside of my mother during one of her admissions. When she was alive, I stayed every night that she was in the hospital to help monitor her and maintain her safety. It's also scary being sick and away from your loved ones. She had chest tubes, IV lines, catheters and oxygen devices with dementia. My biggest concern was for her safety.

My prayer is that all of the patients currently in the hospitals remain safe and get out as soon as possible. Only the sick will get a bed these days. With the CDC Covid-19 Isolation guidelines, families cannot come inside the hospitals and facilities to be at the bedside of their loved ones. The goal is for everyone to be at home as much as possible and wear mask when in public. COVID-19 is a disease that we are still learning how it spreads, the severity of illness it causes, and to what extent it may spread in the United States.

Find ways to deal with not being able to be with your loved one

1. We need to have a clear coping plan – someone to talk to and share how you are feeling
2. Acknowledge that grieving is more challenging at this time – we are in a Health Crisis
3. Deal with stress –write a letter, journal your feelings, exercise, meditate, take a walk, pray, talk to someone
4. Practice self-compassion – be kind to yourself, don't criticize yourself, understand you can only do your part
5. Don't blame self for things out of your control
6. Stay connected via phone, text, or social media if you are grieving and socially isolated, set appointed times to meet with family, friends, or professionals and keep your appointments
7. Find a hobby you can do to occupy your time, make plans for future events of what you would like to do
8. Cut back on watching TV and the constant reports on the news – news increases stress

Make a plan for if you get sick

1. Keep important phone numbers readily available – post on refrigerator:
   • Friends

- Family
- Physician
- Neighbors

2. Limit visitors to your home and keep away from people who are sick.

3. Determine who can care for you if your caregiver gets sick-have a back-up plan.
   - Ask Healthcare Provider about having a 90-day supply of needed medications mailed to avoid going and standing in pharmacy lines.

4. Stock over-the-counter medicines and medical supplies to have on hand to treat fever and/or cold-like symptoms.

5. Stock extra household items and groceries to have on hand if you have to stay at home.

6. Have a plan for someone to care for your children and/or pets if you get ill.

7. Wash your hands often, clean and disinfect frequently touched surfaces.

8. Take everyday precautions to keep space between yourself and others - stay
   Six-feet away, which is about two arm lengths.

Feeling Helpless – Help Someone Else

Feeling helpless can leave us with a feeling of paralysis. Forced to deal with being separated from our loved ones by itself is depressing. Not being involved in their care or allowed to be at the bedside, adds the emotions of helplessness to the list of emotions experienced during the stages of grief. The coronavirus pandemic has turned our world upside-down, leaving people lost, scared, overwhelmed and at times defeated. Feeling helpless right now is totally normal. As humans, we like to think we have power over our lives. When we're robbed of that, it can be unsettling. So, find something to do.

Research has found many examples of how doing good, in ways big or small, not only feels good, but also does us good. Consider the positive feelings you experienced the last time when you did something good for someone else. Helping others is not only good for them and a good thing to do, it also makes us happier and healthier too. Giving also connects us to others, creating stronger communities and helping to build a happier society for everyone. We can give our time, ideas and energy. So, if you want to feel good, do Good!

If you seek an opportunity to help, you shall find:

- Stay home and encourage your loved ones to do the same
- Practice washing your hands, limit touching your face, encourage other to do the same.
- Support local businesses
- Donate to a Food banks
- Clean out garage, basement or closets and give away items
- Send messages of encouragement to people on frontline to let them know you appreciate their service.
- Send a friendly "Hello" to people who mean much to you.
- Check on an elderly neighbor to see if they need anything
- Tap into your creative side of brain – create
- Do something special for yourself
- Pray – Prayer goes where we can't go

Remain Optimistic

As the coronavirus health crisis continues, many of us are struggling to find some sense of normalcy in our daily lives that may reflect a previous time before COVID-19. The daily headlines can be overwhelming with the statistics of deaths and serious illnesses occurring from the virus. We must remain optimistic and continue to follow the CDC guidelines concerning social distancing, wearing masks, gloves, washing of hands, cleaning frequently touched surfaces, and use of hand sanitizers.

The CDC does recommend getting the vaccine first to healthcare workers who are on the front line. The purpose is to help prevent the healthcare worker from getting and spreading the virus that causes COVID-19, to vulnerable people with weakened immune systems. The experts believe that it can help keep you from getting seriously ill. Continued studies about the effect of COVID-19 vaccination on severity of illness from COVID-19, as well as its ability to keep people from spreading the virus that causes COVID-19 are being conducted. The vaccine will help protect you by creating an antibody (immune system) response without having to experience sickness. They do not know how long it will take for the vaccine to start detecting the virus and attacking it from causing sickness.

It is reported that you do not get the live virus. That is a fear to a lot of people. They do not want to have to get the virus injected into them, to prevent them from getting COVID-19. We are all going to have to do our part by continuing to wear our masks, wash our hands and maintain social distancing until we learn more about how to decrease the spread of the virus and find a cure for those infected with serious illnesses. We do not have a full-proof way of knowing 100% whether or not the vaccine is the way to go, but we must remain optimistic and continue to believe that help is on the way.

Although previous pandemics have affected the world before, we have to learn to ride the wave of change and remain positive.

5

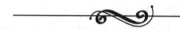

EMOTIONAL TRAUMA AND FINANCIAL RUINS

Just as
Devastating as Physical Illnesses

WHEN WE THINK of the term grief and loss, we often focus on death, dying or illness. However, many people have suffered emotional trauma and financial ruins that have been just as devastating that may have resulted from natural disasters such as some of the World's deadliest tornados, causing the death of thousands of people destroying entire cities. When you lose your home or business, it can be devastating and depressing leaving you feeling helpless, perhaps making you want to quit everything altogether. This is just another area where we can find grief.

When a natural disaster strikes, working with Disaster Relief Organizations help most directly. One of the most effective ways to help is to donate to local disaster relief organizations, as they are familiar with the community and know what resources are readily available. The Red Cross is one of the major Organizations available to provide shelter, food and comfort to families when a disaster occurs. Remember, your donation helps the Red Cross provide shelter, food and comfort to families.

We all have heard of people being subjected to schemes that have wrecked the lives of people financially. I have known several friends who lost their life savings, homes and businesses due to trusting people who violated their trust. Sometimes it's the people we know, love and trust the most, who have the potential to violate us the most. Other times, it is poor judgement, being afraid to say no, or fear of what a person may say or think about us. Nevertheless, anyone can be a subject to a scheming individual or an untrustworthy person. The world is full of them.

There are people that prey upon the generosity of others. There is no full-proof way of knowing 100% whether or not someone is going to be trustworthy. We are only human. We want to trust, but when our trust is determined by what people say instead of what they do, we may fall prey and become a victim. Whether it is intentional or accidental that we lose things that are valuable to us, it hurts. It can be painful. It can also cause us to become angry at the people who caused the major loss or angry at ourselves.

I have learned to pray before making major decisions. I do not allow people to pressure me into doing anything when it comes to making important decisions. Until I have peace about any major decision, I have learned to sit quietly and wait patiently for directions in which way I should go. Even in the face of financial doom and gloom, we see people overcome significant losses and come back strong again.

A good friend of mine had built a large, successful company over the years. He trusted the employees that he had put in positions to run his business. He thought he was financially stable, only to find out that he was bankrupt due to the illegal activities of his trusted staff. They misappropriated millions of dollars from him and caused him to lose everything he had worked hard to build.

After he mourned his losses, he found the strength to rebuild his business by focusing on what he had left versus all he had lost. He had knowledge and experience that could never be taken away from him. He implemented newer technology and new process innovation integration for his company. He opened his mind to allow new ideas, where he had once been closed minded. The tragedy wiped out the old way of doing business and opened him to compete with a competitive advantage utilizing new technology.

He admits that he did not feel better right away, but the process started with him changing his thoughts about how he felt about his current situation. He had to appreciate and recognize what he had left. He found his strength from remembering previous victories and accepting change as inevitable. His company is now worth twice as much as it was previously. He experienced emotional trauma and financial ruins from the people he trusted. He put processes in place to help better monitor his business finances.

He wanted to retaliate on those who had deceived him, but he was reminded of the biblical scripture that says "Vengeance is mine, I will repay, saith the Lord", Romans 12:19. They all received their corresponding punishment as it pertained to the crimes committed. He chose the higher road and let justice prevail. I am sure, many can attest to similar situations.

6

DISTURBING THE DEAD
WITH YOUR GRIEVING

DURING A CONVERSATION with my sister, approximately a month after mom was buried, she shared with me she had seen my mother in a dream. Mom had returned back home. She described mom as looking worn and exhausted, dirty, sick and tired. She had black spots and holes in her feet, and dark circles around her eyes. She basically said she looked very bad. Her diseased body was evident with her sunken face, mottled skin, sagging on her bones. When my brother asked her why was she looking so rugged, she tried to explain to him that she had been laying in her grave with no circulation. She explained to him that her body was decomposed.

During the dream, my mom announced that she would come back to us if it would help us to heal our grieving hearts, and if we wanted her back that much. She said that we were disturbing her rest with all of our grieving and frequent comments about wishing that she was still here with us.

My sister said she saw herself whispering in my ear saying, *"I will give her back to you just as she is now, in this dilapidated condition if you want her"*. Then, as my sister continued to lean over me, as I laid stretched out on the bed, she whispered again telling me, "Don't pull on mama – she is ok, you are waking her up and disturbing her when you continue to cry and grieve for her. She is at rest. She is at peace". Mama then faded away.

I came home the next day feeling very sad. I was processing that my mother was actually gone. I was still mourning. I was angry and I hated to hear that someone else was celebrating the birthday of their loved one who was in their late 80's to 90's. I felt that I should have had my mother another ten or fifteen years. She was so alive and active. It just didn't seem fair. We didn't know why the cancer was there. My mom hated what the cancer had done to her. She was determined to go, so I had to be grateful for the time we did have with her. My emotions still remain up and down, but I don't dare wish her back at this time.

Believers Who Have Died

[13]"But I would not have you to be ignorant, brethren, concerning them which are asleep, that ye sorrow not, even as others which have no hope. [14]For if we believe that Jesus died and rose again, even so them also which sleep in Jesus will God bring with him. [15]For this we say unto you by the word of the Lord, that we which are alive and remain unto the coming of the Lord shall not prevent them which are asleep. [16]For the Lord himself shall descend from heaven with a shout, with the voice of the archangel, and with the trump of God: and the dead in Christ shall rise first: [17]Then we which are alive and remain shall be caught up together with them in the clouds, to meet the Lord in the air: and so shall we ever be with the Lord. [18]Wherefore comfort one another with these words". Thessalonians 4:13-18

<u>MOM YOU WILL BE MISSED</u>

We were blessed to have had you as
our mother for over 60 years,
You took excellent care of us, through
your blood shed and tears.
It wasn't always easy to provide for all our needs,
But you did your very best using all your blessings indeed.
You ran a very tight ship with an ironclad hand,
You always reminded us you were "the
mother" and made us understand,
The reason for your strictness, was
to ensure we did not stray,
You wanted nothing, but the best for
us only to walk right and pray.
You taught us right from wrong and taught us how to pray,
You showed us by example how to live right each day.
The Word specifically tells us to honor our mother and dad,
We were obedient and eager to do so, happily and glad.
We loved you mother dearly, as we cared for you each day,
Yet, you were called to heaven, even
though we wanted you to stay.
Your work here was done, Congratulations, you did it well!
Your legacy will live on through us
as our life stories will tell.

We witnessed His miracle working Power
as He kept you through it all,
He showed us if we trust Him, he would never let us fall.
You loved your family, your church, your
Pastor and Club Members too,
You loved everyone and always did whatever you could do.
You were more than a mother, you were everything to me,
You were my best friend, my teacher
and anything I needed you to be.
Mom you will be missed so much more than I can ever say,
I look forward to our reunion in Heaven one day.
Written by Your Daughter

King Saul Disturbs the Dead by asking
a Medium to Speak with Spirit of the Dead

My sister later reminded me of the biblical story about Saul talking with Samuel's Ghost. Saul was the first king of the United Kingdom of Israel. Prior to Samuel's death, Saul had been trying to get rid of everyone who spoke with the spirits of the dead. But one day the Philistines brought their soldiers together to attack Israel. When Saul took one look at the Philistine army, he started shaking with fear. He reached out to ask the Lord what to do. The Lord did not answer him either in a dream, or by a priest or a prophet.

Saul decided to seek the advice of a Medium, someone who could talk to the spirits of the dead. He wanted to know what was going to happen. He wanted to know if he was going to win or lose the battle. In the past, he had relied on the counsel and wisdom of Samuel for all advice. Now he, himself was seeking someone who could talk with the dead for his own benefit. He disguised himself as he sought out a woman known for talking to the spirits of the dead. The woman was afraid of him as she discerned that Saul was the king who had promised to kill everyone who was doing the very thing that he was asking her to do. He swore to her that she would not be killed.

When she conducted the séance, to bring up the ghost of Samuel, he asked, Saul why was he bothering him having this lady bring him up like this. Saul told him that he was terribly worried that he was about to be attacked by the Philistines and God has seemed to turn his back on him. He told Samuel that God won't answer him any more by prophets or by dreams. He asked what should he do?

Samuel said:

"If the Lord has turned away from you and is now your enemy, don't ask me what to do. I've already told you: The Lord has sworn to take the kingdom from you and give it to David. And that's just what he's doing!

When the Lord was angry with the Amalekites, he told you to destroy them, but you didn't do it. That's why the Lord is doing this to you. Tomorrow the Lord will let the Philistines defeat Israel's army, then you and your sons will join me down here in the world of the dead". Saul and his sons died that next day and joined Samuel in the world of the dead as he had told him in the séance. 1 Samuel 28: 16-19 (CEV)

I read an article by a Medium on Disturbing the Dead – Why Would a Spiritual Medium Do That? The author says "Our loved ones in the spirit world want to contact us, they want to communicate and talk. They want to be remembered, some of them want to find peace". I am all for remembering our loved ones and keeping their memory alive. I also believe that we may have visits from them from time to time, because their soul lives on, only their bodies die. However, I don't agree that we should be calling out for those spirits to come forth once they have passed on. If they have found peace leave them alone.

When my sister shared her visionary dream-like encounter with me, I immediately said "Deuces mama, I will let you rest". I knew without a shadow of doubt that I did not want mama coming back in the deteriorated condition that had been displayed in the dream-like vision. If she was resting and at peace, that was my cue for me to be at peace as well. I didn't want her coming back here in that condition, and I wasn't ready to join her in the world of the dead either. You can say I was scared straight and ceased to grieve for the time being.

I shared with her that I believed that I was led to write a book about grief and overcoming the loss with strength. I remember starting off talking very strong and confident about how I would be used to write "From Grief to Strength" to help people all over the world. I was so excited. Immediately after I had spoken, I thought, "who do you think you are, you're nobody to be able to make a statement like that".

"The thief cometh not, but for to steal, and to kill, and to destroy: I am come that they might have life, and that they might have _it_ more abundantly." John 10:10

We must remember, anytime we decide to take a stand and believe for a miracle, the enemy will not sit back without a fight. We must be ready to stand firm on the Word, because He promised us victory.

I immediately started to take back what I had just proclaimed and started to agree with the inner thought. I began to correct myself and started to look at myself in the natural. I thought to myself and almost agreed with the thought and begin to ask myself, "How in the world can I make a difference in the lives of people all over the world?" I didn't realize that I had actually said "the world". I didn't want to sound like I was coming across in our conversation that I was about to do something on this grand scale on my own from a few little stories written on a piece of paper. It just came out of my mouth. My sister said, "You can do whatever you want to do to help people, if you believe that you can do it".

I immediately began to cast down that thought, as I recognized that it was contradicting the vision in my spirit. It was the enemy. That's his job to try to talk us out of believing that we can do great things if we believe that we can. I said right, "If God is for us, who can be against us? Romans 8:31. I realized that I don't need a string of spiritual credentials to write a book to comfort people.

I only need my Creator to be with me and to speak His powerful words". He said, "Follow your dream, because I will certainly be with you. My job is to trust Him and He will supply whatever I need". I am called to make a difference beyond myself to help others.

**"I can do all things through Christ
which strengtheneth me."
Phillipians 4:13**

52

7

MY STORY

Daily Meditation for Guidance

I SAT IN my chair by the window in my bedroom, overlooking the beautiful, blossoming trees blowing in the wind with the warm sun beaming down on me during my morning meditation. I prayed for guidance and direction for my day as I generally do. I learned if I start my day with prayer and meditation, I can prioritize the long list of things that I always seem to have to do. When we take time out to spend time in meditation, we can get instructions for our day to be more productive. When we quiet our minds with meditation, we can receive directions, instructions and reminders.

Perhaps we left may have left lights on, doors unlocked, coffee pots or irons still plugged into the wall socket or our lunch still in the refrigerator. When we set our priorities, we don't waste time on things that could wait and ensure that we do what is most important.

I am a Registered Nurse who is on the front line, currently taking care of patients who have tested positive for the COVID-19 virus. I work the night shift, but during this pandemic, I have had to be extremely flexible, to cover various positions in our organization, for staff and administrators, in their absence due to a lot of them being plagued with the COVID-19 Virus.

I have had to work extremely long, stressful days and nights. Yet and still, I prayed what more could I do to help during this Coronavirus Pandemic. I know that I am called to make a difference in the lives of others beyond what I can do myself.

Although nursing is very stressful during this time, it is critical that I stay focused, get plenty of rest and pray more than ever. I pray for my own safety, my family and friends. I pray for my patients as they mourn not having their families at their bedside. I pray for my pastor, other ministers, leaders in our state and local government, for our country and all over the world.

My prayers go out across the healthcare continuum as they struggle to provide adequate staffing, equipment, vaccines, technology, and integrate various healthcare services so that continuum can be successfully managed for those in need of care. My prayer goes out to everyone else on the front line keeping this economy going as well. We are all affected by this treacherous, deadly virus. I am praying for an end to this pandemic and strength for those directly affected though devastating losses. May God bless and keep those who are still here.

My Story Continues

I sat in my bedroom, I listened until I heard, "Write a book". I initially said, who am I to write a book? I then asked "what would I write about, where do I start?" I was reminded of all of the sickness I witnessed while caring for my patients, their family and friends, and the tons of tragedies that came through the emergency room doors and on the streets that I had grown up on. I was reminded of my own share of pain and grief. It was at that point, I decided to call the book,

"From Grief to Strength". I said, ok Lord, I will do whatever you would have me to do if it will help somebody else's life to be better.

I was eager to write, but immediately, became hesitant when I was led to include stories about myself. I thought, it's easier to write stories about other people. I added, plus this is not an autobiography. We don't get to make the rules. Our job is to obey. I had my reasons for my reluctance, as you will see later. Nevertheless, fear is never a reason to be disobedient.

We hear about tragedies every day. There are thousands of programs on television that are dedicated to solving crimes and tragic stories of all types of situations. A lot of them are based on real life situations. I have actually watched a few of those programs and seen stories that I had personal knowledge of. It can be scary to think that bad things can happen to good people, even when you are trying to do the right thing. These programs can make you feel terrified and unsafe in the most secure environment, because a lot of these tragedies occur behind the same locked doors where you are supposed to feel safe.

Growing up, I recall several people, who died horrible deaths from the violence in the neighborhood. We lived across the hall from a large drug operation. I recall my family having to enter the building where we lived, greeted by soldiers holding machine guns. We had to get permission to go into our own apartment. There were many times we had to lay down on the floor to avoid being hit by bullets flying over our heads, as the war on drugs prevailed. Many of our childhood friends, grew up to be drug dealers or drug addicts. My mom was a victim of domestic violence. She was determined to get us out of that neighborhood, so that we could have a better life. She did not settle for the hand she was dealt as a divorced mother with little children. I grieved the loss of my dad and the breakdown of our family unit.

We moved several times having to leave friends and schools behind. I learned to adjust to new environments and meet new friends along the way. We always went to church and was taught to pray and love one another. We were poor, but we were happy. I participated in sport activities, sang in glee clubs, ran track, and excelled in academics. I graduated high school and attended the local community college. It was there that I was attacked off campus on my way home from class. I was snatched off the street at gun point, tied up, gagged, blind-folded, raped and robbed. I was left in an alley, in the rain, in the dark with rats and grass as tall as I was. I was terrified and tormented. I was taken to the local emergency room where I was further humiliated by the staff and police. I was only 19 years old. I did not get a chance to process the pain and trauma for many years, because I did not get the counseling I needed at the time. Holding that kind of pain inside of me was doing more damage than I had any idea that it was doing.

I join the military and got a job. I graduated from college, as a Registered Nurse, and work for many years helping others. I had underlying anger issues and an alcohol dependency addiction. You could not have told me that at the time, but my behavior said otherwise and led me into some very dark places.

I blacked-out one night and was told that I had shot my ex-boyfriend. I did not remember the details of the incident, but it cost me 6 years in prison.

He refused to speak to me prior to my sentencing and told the judge that I was calling and harassing him. He was angry and only wanted to hurt me. The judge threatened to revoke my bond and lock me up and wait in jail for sentencing if I tried to reach out to him again. So, I never got a chance to apologize to him before my sentencing. Several months into my sentence, I wrote him a letter and apologized for shooting him. I asked him for forgiveness and he said he forgave me. Fortunately for us both, he did not die and forgave me. He later told me that he had set me up, because I did not want to marry him at that time. That was very painful. He tried to recant his statement, but once the gavel hits the bench, that sentence is yours to completion.

If I had never been taken out of my life, I would have never known that such a world existed. My time behind the bars was an eye-opening experience. It was another world within a world. Believe it or not, I am grateful for that experience. I did not want to go for the obvious reasons, but mainly due to the fact I had just had a baby girl. I had waited my entire adult life to get married and have a baby, only to have to give her up for someone else to raise in my absence. All of my life I wanted to have a child. I was told by doctors that I would never give birth to a child. I had to leave my only daughter behind. Fortunately, I had a sister who took her in and raised her in my absence.

As I look back now, I can see the many blessings that came from that experience. I was able to give my sister an opportunity to be a mother. She was unable to have children of her own. She loved my daughter as her very own. I could not have left her in better hands. My daughter was raised in a stable, Christian home shared by my sister and her wonderful husband. They instilled good morals and values into my daughter that has kept her grounded in Christ.

"Train up a child in the way he should go: and when he is old, he will not depart from it". **Proverbs 22:6**

Knowing that my daughter was in good hands, I did not worry about her. I knew they would do their best to keep her safe and take excellent care of her. A lot of women did not have that secure feeling about where their children were. With my daughter being in good hands, that allowed me to help the disadvantaged women maintain their parental rights. I worked as a Paralegal in the Law Library and fought for the women. Many of them had various healthcare issues and was in need of medical treatment that had been denied. I fought for medications, surgeries, equipment, and various medical procedures to be done. I remember one incident where an inmate had been complaining of a headache for several months. She was given Tylenol and send her back to her cell.

One day, the inmate passed out and had a seizure. The healthcare personnel left her on the floor until the seizure was over. I knew this inmate needed medical attention, I filed a medical grievance on her behalf, and demanded that medical treatment be granted to her. They finally did a CT scan of her brain and found a tumor that required immediate surgery. They allowed an Intern to practice doing this delicate surgical procedure on her brain. A huge mistake was made, paralyzing the inmate. Many people believe that the incarcerated lives are disposable and do not matter. I saw so many women suffer needlessly, because the prison delayed medical treatment for new onsets, and only provided basic care to those with preexisting medical problems.

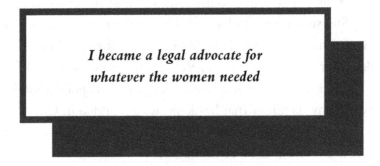

I became a legal advocate for whatever the women needed

During that time, I helped sentences to be reversed, early releases to be granted, cases to be dismissed and/or thrown out, inmate tickets dismissed, divorces decreed, and child custody cases reversed. I started exercise programs, bible studies and even hosted revivals. I got a chance to exercise my faith and lead a lot of women to Christ. It was an exciting time.

I became the Editor of the newspaper and started a column for Spiritually Articles. Our newspaper went all over the United States into other prison facilities. I got responses from many readers. I also incorporated "Gotcha" snap shots. We took the camera around the facility grounds and took pictures of inmates. This boosted their morale. I wrote articles of their achievements and news worthy events. Everyone looked forward to the newspaper. We also had a section where I interviewed "Lifers" These women had life sentences, but found a way to live a productive life behind the bars. The Sentencing Project and other organizations worked closely with overturning sentences for many of those women as well.

During my time of incarceration, I developed a very close relationship with my Heavenly Father. I read the bible from cover to cover several times. I participated in church services, bible studies. I helped so many women not lose their children and whatever they needed me to do. I loved my job. The prisoners thought I was staff. I made the best of my situation and adapted to the new way of life that I had been granted.

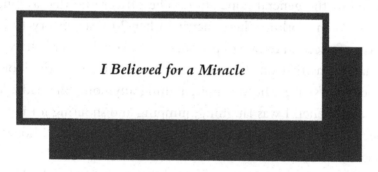

I Believed for a Miracle

I made arrangements for my sister to come to the state where I was incarcerated to complete my legal business one month after I had been incarcerated. I vividly recall boldly standing in faith. I was believing to be allowed to get out of the 30-day quarantine early to be able to visit with my daughter when my sister came to court for me. I had a cellmate who was an atheist. She did not believe in God. I did not want my court date to be changed, so I chose to believe, by faith, to have my time in quarantine cut short. I wanted to see my three-month old daughter.

The day came and I was packed and ready to go. I waited for my name to be called at the 11:00 am scheduled Friday call to release prisoners to go out into the general population. I needed to be out, because no visits were allowed during quarantine period. The officer called all of the names on the list except mine. I was shocked. I knew I had heard in my spirit that I would be released on that day. I was sad for a moment, but mostly annoyed by my cellmate who had been mocking me for the entire time about believing for my miracle. She laughed and belly-rolled around on the floor, saying "I told you that you are wasting your time". She kept laughing, saying "ah ha, you're not going anywhere, look at all those meals you missed for nothing" by fasting. She wouldn't stop laughing. I finally told her to "stop talking to me, the day wasn't over yet". I resumed praying and praising for my miracle. I sang praises and continued to rejoice in the face of my cellmate.

At 4pm, another call was made for a few more people to be released to the general population. The officer said that as long as she had been working there, never in her 20-year history had she known of a second release of prisoners. Yes, you'd better believe that my name was first on that list. You should have seen the look on my cellmate's face. She was not laughing anymore. She had a look of total disbelief. I was laughing, jumping and shouting for joy, as I collected my packed bags and left. I told my cellmate, "I hope you can see that my faith is real and He does answer prayers".

I was all prepared for my visit. I called my family and told them I was out and they could come visit early. However, on Monday there was a gas leak and nobody could come in or out of the facility. All visits were cancelled. I went to see my counselor the next day to tell her that I missed my visit due to the emergency that occurred on the previous day. She yelled and screamed at me and told me too bad, get out of her office. Only high security leveled prisoners were allowed to visit on Tuesdays. She told me to tell them to come back on Wednesday, which was the next visiting day. I told her that my sister had brought my daughter from out of state, and they had to fly back on Tuesday night. She slammed her door in my face and told me to get away from her door. I walked away crying, totally distraught. I cried out asking "why was I allowed to get out early for a visit I believed was promised to me?" Why did the counselor slam the door in my face?

As I walked away sobbing and crying, I felt in my spirit to go back to the counselor and tell her that I cannot take no for an answer". I looked around to see if someone else was talking to me. I realized I had to be obedient and turn around, go back and say what I felt in my spirit. I wiped my tears away enough to see my way back to her office. I reluctantly knocked on her door. She snatched the door open and yelled, "What do you want?" I opened my mouth and said, I said, "I can't take no for an answer". These were Spirit-filled words. I did not say it with any authority, because I was still crying and barely able to get the words out. She just stood there looking at me in disbelief. She told me to hold on. She slammed the door in my face again. When she opened it again, she said "your daughter will be here in two hours. I have cancelled all high security level visits until your visit with your daughter is over". I was granted the entire visiting room for my visit with my daughter and my sister. Everything had been moved around to make sure that my visit that I had believed for was honored. My prayer request was answered. James 5:16 says "The effectual fervent prayer of a righteous man availeth much."

I believed for that 30th day in June. I stood on the Word until my miracle came to pass. I was obedient to speak to the counselor even when it did not make sense to me in the natural.

I was taught to listen to the still small voice and trust wholeheartedly. The adversary did everything he could to try to stop me, but as long as I kept my eyes focused on the promise, it was nothing that could be done to stop the promise to me. This was just one of the many miracles performed in my life.

I believe when we personally witness miracles, it strengthens our faith. The bible is full of miracles performed to help non-believers believe. Miracles continues to be performed every day, if we just believe. I shared this story to reflect the power of immovable faith. If we will only trust and believe, our pain, suffering, and circumstances will be moved away. We just need to have faith and believe.

I fought for so many women and helped them to get out, but all of my own appeals were denied. I watched women die and kill themselves, because they lost all hope. I shared the gospel to those who would listen. I completed my sentence then returned back home. All of the practice I had fighting for the women, paid off when I wrote my petition to the Board of Nursing to reinstate my nursing license. I had to fight twice as hard to get my life back in order. I jumped through hundreds of hoops and loops, but I had the faith to believe. I got my nursing license back. I had been told that I would never practice nursing again. They did not know, that I cannot lose anything that belongs to me by divine right; I am under my Master's Grace; and not under law. It is my divine right to have whatever I say I can have.

I thought it was hard leaving my daughter, but it was even harder to get her back. She wanted to stay with the only parents she had ever known. That was hard for me to grasp, even though I understood. I was selfish and wanted what I wanted. I took my daughter away against her will. I figured she would adjust and eventually love me, because I was her biological mother. I had to return her to my sister, because I saw how unhappy she was. I was devastated, but I had to try to understand. I had to accept my situation and learn to live as harmonious as I could possibly live with my situation. I prayed a lot and got angry, but I eventually realized that I should be grateful that I had someone to love and care for my daughter as much as I did.

I was later told that I had taken on the responsibility of mending the gap between myself and my daughter, leaving my Lord out altogether. He told me that if I had trusted Him to handle the entire situation from day one, all this grief could have been avoided. He said all I had to do was to ask Him to help bridge the gap between myself and my daughter and he would have done it. He said you never opened your mouth to ask for my help. You cried for two years to anyone who would listen to you. None of them could do a thing about it. They eventually got tired of hearing me whine and cry about the same thing and quit taking my calls. Talking about grief.

I have learned that every experience we have fits into a pattern for good, to those who love the Lord. Nothing is wasted when we walk by faith. Even our mistakes and sins can be used for something good.

8

BEING THANKFUL AND GRATEFUL IS THE KEY

I STAYED IN the same house as my sister and her husband to get to know my daughter for most of the first year after returning home. I had missed the first six years of her life. Had I not insisted and forced my own way, our relationship would have been healed sooner. We have free will. Either we trust or we keep bumping our heads and causing more pain, until we surrender. We must cast our cares over unto the Lord, for He truly cares for us. I knew what I was supposed to do, but I took matters into my own hands, and wasted many more years trying to do things on my own. I wasn't truly grateful for the generosity of my sister and her husband offering to help bridge the gap between myself and my daughter. I wanted them to support what I wanted to do and how I wanted to do it. Apparently, we did not have the same vision. I moved out and took my daughter again. Only to return her once again. We definitely could have benefited from some serious counseling. We must be open to receive help, when we are grieving and adjusting to new life changes.

Shortly, thereafter, I met a young, married mother with several little children. She developed a fever, went into a coma, and suffered multi-system organ failure, causing her body to go into shock. She had some type of rare blood infection that caused her to have to have both hands and feet amputated. When she woke up from her coma, she had to be told that she lost her hands and feet. The screams that came from her could have awaken the dead. It was one of the worse cries I had ever experienced. She was overwhelmed with grief, and rightly so. I had been praying while she was in the coma for something encouraging to say to her when she woke up. I cried for her during that time. Pondering how I could help her situation, gave me a totally different perspective in regards to my own situation. I had cried for two consecutive years over a situation that wasn't nearly close to what this young mother was facing. Suddenly, all of my tears were gone. I was not crying for me anymore. I felt ashamed for even wasting tears and feeling sorry for myself unnecessarily. When I reached out to help her, I was able to heal and move on with my own life. I had been so focused on me, that I could not see that real problems were occurring all around me. I was so blessed and could not see it.

> **I wasted time focusing on the negative things and complaining about what I did not have, instead of focusing on what I did have.**

I immediately repented for my selfishness. I prayed and asked for something to say to her to help her to have a glimpse of hope. I wanted to help and was willing to do whatever I could to help that young couple. My prayers were answered and I was able to comfort her momentarily. I researched and found another couple who had experienced the same devastating tragedy of losing both upper and lower limbs. What a miracle. They were able to connect and be support for each other. What were the odds of finding another young couple dealing with the exact same medical issues at the exact same time? It was truly a blessing for all of them. Nobody could relate to them like they could relate to each other. She eventually went home after spending months in an Acute Rehabilitation facility. She got prosthetic hands and feet during her therapy. She sent pictures back waving, smiling and holding her beautiful children in her arms. That was my prayer for her. She overcame her tragedy triumphantly.

9

RECOVERY AFTER ADDICTION IS POSSIBLE

BY THE TIME Gina was only 15 years old, she was already addicted to heroin. Her innocence had been taken away by a local drug dealing, guy who preyed on children. He was well known to everyone in the neighborhood as the "Guy with the Goods". They called him Big G. If you needed something, Big G either had it, or could get it. It was easy to trust him, because he always came across as a friendly guy who would give candy and/or spare change to the children. He was also known as the guy who would help the poor, struggling, single moms in the neighborhood. Later, they would find out that they would owe him for his seemingly genuine generosity.

Many young mothers got caught up in his web of deceit. They found themselves doing things that they never thought they would do. Their homes became trap houses used by local drug dealers to exchange not only drugs and money, but sexual favors in exchange for the help rendered. He offered them a way to make a little extra money for themselves. He basically set them up for prostitution. Many of the low self-esteemed women became a part of a vicious cycle that would later extend to their little innocent children.

Gina was the oldest of her mother's five children. She was smart and beautiful. I met her when we were 14 years old. I had been transferred to a high school on the other side of town. She welcomed me and we became friends. She showed me around, but she never told me about her secret life of drugs and affiliations. She seemed normal and did well in school. She told me that she was her mother's little helper. I never thought any more about it, because she seemed so comfortable with her role.

When, her mother became addicted to the drugs that Joe was peddling, she began to look after her siblings and took on the role of mothering for them. She was forced to grow up and deal with adult responsibilities when in fact, she was just a child herself. Joe would always compliment her on how good she looked, how mature she was and how well she took care of her younger siblings. This made Gina feel good that she was stepping up to take care of her family. He began to give her money to buy extra things for her young siblings and fine things for herself. She began to trust him, which was exactly what he wanted her to do.

He later extended her a way to relax from the responsibilities of young motherhood by introducing her to heroin. He taught her how to snort a few lines. He told her it would make her an even better mother figure to her siblings without feeling like she was doing anything extra. She believed him and came to expect the little package that he always seemed to generously gift her with. She had no idea that she was becoming addicted. Her mom was already addicted and had basically abandoned the family altogether. Joe was all Gina had, so she trusted him all the more.

She later began to boost clothes for him. She would go into stores and shoplift for him. They would sell the clothes on the street for a fraction of the cost. People began to place orders for what they wanted and Gina would go into the stores, steal the items and sell them to their customers. She eventually got caught and was sent to jail. This was the beginning of a long career of shoplifting and incarcerations.

Her drug habit increased and she began to use more and more drugs. She became addicted to crack cocaine and heroin. Her life spent out of control. She was in and out of jail. She was no longer able to care for her younger siblings. They were forced to fend for themselves. Gina later had children of her own, two sons and a daughter. She left them with her mother who was barely able to take care of herself. Over the years, Gina had developed a high tolerance to snorting the heroin and needed to inject the drugs directly into her veins to get high. This beautiful young girl spent the next 30 years addicted to the drugs that had been so casually introduced to her, under the pretention of helping her to relax from the responsibilities of motherhood that she had inherited from her own mother. She abandoned her siblings and later her own biological children as well.

Her mother begged her to get her life together and to quit doing drugs. She had a stroke which prevented her from being able to leave the house, where she was forced to kicked the habit of drugs. She told Gina that she was dying of cancer and could no longer care for her children. Gina had tried rehab a few times after being discharged from jail and prison, but she just couldn't seem to kick the habit. Her children hated her and would refuse to deal with her when she would show up to her mother's home to see them after being gone several months at a time. This rejection would send her back to using drugs. It was a vicious cycle. She would say "I want to cut back on my drug use, but I am not ready to quit altogether". Cutting back was not an option, nor was it reality. It would take a real commitment to walk away, before she would experience the miracle.

Finally, after many years of incarceration and numerous felonies later, Gina made the decision that she would get clean and leave the street life behind. She was broken and tired of the vicious cycle that her life was going in. Her mother suffered a massive heart attack after her stroke and died. Gina's small children really needed her. She had to get herself together. She realized that she no longer had the support of her mother to care for her children. She had been bitter for all of those years she was forced to take care of her siblings while her mother was strung out on drugs. She found herself doing the same thing her mother had done to her. She eventually lost her home, when she could no longer pay for it. She and her children were homeless and found themselves on the cold streets of the inner city.

She was taken in by a Christian family who was led to help her. She got clean and sober, went back to school, got a job and has remained clean and sober for the past several years. She had the gruesome task of dealing with her children with whom she had abandoned. Her sons were much more forgiving than her daughter had been. Her daughter was angry. She had several children of her own and left them with Gina to take care of. Her daughter felt that Gina owed her for abandoning her and her brothers. She made her mother pay every chance she got.

Gina desperately tried to make amends with everyone that she had hurt during her addiction, but the challenge of amending her relationship with her children was her greatest challenge of all. Healing would have to come before they could move into a new realm of their relationship. She was determined that she would do whatever it would take to heal their relationship. Eventually, the daughter came around, forgave her mother and now appreciates the family unit as a whole. The grandchildren will benefit by having a stable, drug free home to grow up in.

Gina eventually got married. She was given an incredible opportunity to work as a Program Director of a Community Outreach Center. She was able to give back to her community she once terrorized with her criminal activities. She has a wonderful life and professional career now. She was given this awesome position with the multiple felony convictions on her criminal record. She proved that she was done with her past, by remaining drug free. She became a home owner, a phenomenal mother and gracious grandmother, a committed wife, a trustworthy employee and loyal friend. Gina overcame her life of grief with strength when she made up her mind that she was moving forward and promised never to look back. She remembers the pain and suffering from the drug withdrawals, and anguish she caused her family. She graciously chooses to share her story of triumph to let others know that no life is too far gone. It can be restored. A made-up mind will take you wherever you desire to go and will allow you to do whatever you desire to do. Recovery after addiction is possible. She returned to a normal state of health, mind and strength.

10

REJECTION

REJECTION IS ONE of the most common emotional wounds that we may experience in our daily life. Rejection can come in many forms: breaking up with your boyfriend/girlfriend, being turned down by someone you'd like to get to know, not being accepted into your preferred college or being passed over for job position you really wanted, especially if you are over the age of 40, or just simply not being accepted by your family due to lifestyle choices. Some divorced couples may reject you, when you get a divorce. You become an outcast because of your new social status. Women who don't have children are left out the mother's clubs and sometimes left feeling empty on Mother's Day. With today's technology, our avenues to receive rejection extends past our family, friends and local community, it also extends to social media platforms and dating apps, where someone might ignore our posts, chats, texts, or dating profiles leaving us with the feeling of being rejected. Regardless of what form it make come in, rejection is a horrible feeling. We all get our heart-broken at least once in this lifetime by one of the avenues listed or some other form.

Just like grief, you're dealing with the loss of losing something that you had your heart set on. Most of rejection is based on how we perceive it. Rejection is emotional pain that can impact our well-being. It can damage our mood and our self-esteem. We can become angry and become unstable in our need to belong.

The best way to boost feelings of self-worth after a rejection is to affirm positive aspects about yourself. We must remind ourselves that we are loved and appreciated and point out the good things we like about ourselves to help feel better about ourselves. We can seek out new relationships and associate with people who do support and appreciate us. I always say, "I would much rather spend my time with people who celebrate me, versus those who only tolerate me".

I had a patient who attempted to commit suicide, because he thought he had tested positive for COVID-19. In his mind, that was a death sentence, so he jumped off a bridge, broke several bones, got hit by a car and survived. He later found out that he was negative. He told me that he believed his family would reject him due to his positive COVID-19 status. Rejection comes in all forms.

A female from my military unit was devastated by the rejection of a broken relationship. Her depression was heavy and our Commander placed her on suicide watch. All she talked about was how hurt she was that her relationship was over with her boyfriend. She could not focus on anything else, to include her personal hygiene. I remember someone saying, "Get over it and get another one, forget about him." It was easy for someone on the outside to make such insensitive comments, because they did not understand how deeply, disturbed she was.

She had personalized the breakup and blamed herself. She felt that losing him would ruin the rest of her life. She could not see that the pain would not last forever. We took turns guarding her while we were on our two-week tactical training exercise. We made it through the training and she told us that she appreciated all of our attempts to comfort her. She said she felt better and the Commander released her from suicide watch. I always felt that she never should have been released, based on the fact that she said she felt better, but should have been sent directly to a psychiatric center to be professionally evaluated. All threats of suicide should be taken seriously.

Upon returning to our city, it was reported that she jumped from a bridge into the river and killed herself. I always thought, how terribly sad she must have been, to believe that there was no hope for her. I pray that no one will ever feel that hopelessness again in life about any situation. I believe that talking to a professional about your feelings can help you to see a better way of dealing with whatever crisis you may be facing. Always take the threat of suicide seriously. Encourage the person to call a suicide hotline number. In the U.S., call the National Suicide Prevention Lifeline at 800-273-TALK (800-273-8255) to reach a trained counselor. With support, people can heal and regain the ability to move forward in their lives. It doesn't have to end tragically.

We must be kind to ourselves and not be afraid to reach out for help. Some cultures think asking for help indicates you are admitting weakness, defeat, or may dredge up feelings of shame and guilt. Not asking for help can be detrimental to your health. Although this young lady did not have victory over her circumstance in this situation, I included it in an effort to prevent someone else who may be thinking all hope is gone. I want you to know that there is hope. There is help. Reach out and get it so that you will triumph over the situation.

Not everyone will take rejection to that extreme, but it can be very painful. I watched a documentary where scientists placed people in a magnetic resonance imaging machine, (MRI), which is a type of scan that uses strong magnetic fields and radio waves to produce detailed images of the inside of the body. The people were asked to recall a situation when they had been rejected. It was discovered that the same areas of the brain became illuminated as when they had actually experienced the physical pain. The memory of the rejection was just as vivid as the actual time of rejection. So, the thoughts of pain, must be replaced by thoughts of positive experience. We must not linger in the pain, as it can remain alive as long as we continue to focus on the painful situation.

Rejecting the Rejected of Our Society

Imagine the pain someone with a blemished background has to go through. I am speaking of those individuals who have a criminal record. In some states, all you have to have, is an arrest on your record that could have been dismissed. If you ever get a spot on your background record, someone will always attempt to judge you without ever getting to know you or the skills you could possibly bring to the table.

Our society says someone with a clean background is a better choice candidate, than someone who has a documented committed crime and has been prosecuted in a court of law for the crime. That is not necessarily so. Some people may have never been caught and may not be the best candidate for the job. There are thousands of people working in all types of professional positions that are methamphetamine addicts, smoke marijuana, snort cocaine, shoot heroine, and drink on the job. Their backgrounds are squeaky clean.

A lot of ex-offenders have paid their dues to society and don't do drugs or drink alcohol. They should be given the chance to re-enter society without having to relive their past, if they qualify. Of course, if someone has been a career criminal and have shown that they would do your business more harm than good, the background record serves as a good tool to determine if that candidate could be a suitable candidate or not. Some employers make a policy that no one with a documented crime on their background will be allowed employment with their company, regardless of the crime. They will not even look at your application. Every business has the right to set selection criteria for their business employment guidelines.

All in all, almost one in every three adults in the United States has the task of explaining a criminal record to prospective employers. Ex-offenders are capable of adding much more value to an employer than the employer may even realize. Employers need to be willing to give ex-offenders a chance, and let them explain that their past does not define who they are today. According to the National Employment Law Project (NELP), 70 million people in America have criminal records.

If you are that candidate, I would recommend that ex-offenders do everything in their power to improve their skill set. Whether it is obtaining a certificate, completing trade school training, or graduating with a highly coveted STEM (science, technology, engineering, and mathematics) college degree, Ex-offenders who invest in themselves will find it much easier to convince hiring managers to extend an offer of employment. Choose to remain positive. Keep trying, don't be discouraged. Someone will offer you a job. If not, tap into your own God given talent and create an opportunity for yourself. I too, have to take my own advice. I still experience rejection for having a blemished background. It is not easy, but you must remain strong and optimistic. You will persevere if you don't give up.

"But if ye forgive not men their trespasses, neither will your Father forgive your trespasses." Matthew 6:15

Parting Thoughts

As I completed the previous chapter, my intentions were to summarize the book contents and close the book, but I was stricken with a house fire that nearly took my life. I was awakened by a house full of flames, as I choked on the smoke. I had fallen asleep cooking breakfast, after working a long night shift. I immediately jumped up and ran to the front door as the flames were gaining on me.

I screamed for my neighbors to call the fire department and prayed that they would arrive soon. I was thankful to have made it out safely. The Fire Marshall asked why I didn't I just jump out the window, instead of running to the front door, towards the flames. He then told me that there had been eight fatalities in my county that day and I was the only one who had made it out safely. I was stricken with sadness for those victims who had died that day in house fires.

A Fireman came to me after the fire had been extinguished carrying my computer from my office. I thought it was strange that he would hand me my flat screen desk top computer, of all things, being that I did not have on any socks or shoes. It was an all-in-one type model, which was light weight. I immediately remembered, and shouted "My Book". I was grateful that my book had not been lost in the fire.

My prayer for the book is to encourage the readers who may be going through a period of grief, sadness, illness, or some other life issue that may have caught you off guard. I hope that some of the contents of this book resonated in your spirit to give you a glimpse of hope, if you were feeling hopeless or a source of comfort if you were experiencing pain. When we know we are not alone, sometimes it may help to lighten the burden. Life crisis seem to never end at times. They just seem to keep coming one situation after another. We may ask, why is this happening to me? Why did I lose my loved one, my job, my family or my friend? Why did the tornado or hurricane hit my community? Why was my loved one murdered, kidnapped, robbed or raped? The list of whys could go on and on.

I asked many of the same questions. My answers came as I pondered the scriptures of my Bible. 2 Corinthians 12:9 says… "And he said unto me, My grace is sufficient for thee: for my strength is made perfect in weakness." Whenever a situation is beyond our control, we must turn it over to a power greater than us. When we are feeling helpless, hopeless, powerless or just distressed about anything, we can find strength to handle the situation. 1 Peter 5:7 says "Casting all your care upon him; for he careth for you."

I have to admit that this book has been healing for my own spirit, as I was inspired to choose the stories that made it to print. Of course, there are millions of stories much more tragic and devastating that I do not know about that you may have experienced. Regardless of which stories were told, the bottom line is, we all experience various types of tragedies, wretched events, or different kinds of grief in our lifetime.

I had to remember that 1 Peter 4:12, says, "Beloved, think it not strange concerning the fiery trial which is to try you, as though some strange thing happened unto you..." I believe when we set out to do Kingdom Work or help others, the enemy is angry, for his job is to kill, steal and destroy. He doesn't want to see you happy, wealthy or strong. He wants to keep you bound by grief, remorse, bitterness, guilt, and every form of bondage that will keep you from living a joyous life. We live in a world that is more spiritual than real. We are in a fight against evil and we are not wrestling against flesh and blood, but against the rulers, over darkness, against spiritual forces of evil in the heavenly places. We are dealing with forces that we cannot see and must fight with spiritual weapons according to the Word.

When I made a commitment to write this book, I knew that I would be attacked. I suffered attacks on my family, my friends, my finances, my home, my job, and anything of concern to me. I had experienced it before and knew enough about standing in faith, until I saw the victory manifested in my life. I had interpersonal relationships come under attack, cancer within my family, division within my family, loss of freedom, loss of loved ones, loss of my businesses, home burned down, total vehicle wrecked in an accident, death of family members and friends. As a result, I lost my enthusiasm to complete this book after the fire, but I had to remind myself of the blessing that I still had the gift of life. It took a while to get motivated again, but I found the strength as I re-read what I had already written and continued to write.

The fiery trials and tribulations that I endured in the past, were all in preparation for me to take a stand today. I have waivered in my faith over the years and have fallen short of being all that I should be many times. When I fell, I got up, I repented and asked for forgiveness. I searched my heart to make sure that I was not harvesting un-forgiveness, bitterness, or resentments in my heart. I got back in position to persevere to the end.

I shared this information, because it is imperative that we walk in love and forgiveness with each other, even in the face of whatever we are going through. We must start with self-forgiveness, self-love and having a grateful attitude. I know that I am blessed, despite all of the attacks in my life over the years. I know that nothing will be wasted. I just stand and continue to watch as I am strengthened through it all.

I boldly confess that I am an overcomer from grief to strength by the power, love, and Grace of God!

IMPORTANT NUMBERS IF YOU NEED HELP OR INFORMATION

- **Grief Share Support Group – GriefShare.org - 800-395-5755 (US and Canada)**
  919-562-2112 (International) Find a support group near you. Email info@griefshare.org
- **SAMHSA's National Helpline,** 1-800-662-HELP (4357), or TTY: 1-800-487-4889 is a confidential, free, 24-hour-a-day, 365-day-a-year, information service, in English and Spanish, for individuals and family members facing mental and/or substance use disorders. This service provides referrals to local treatment facilities, support groups, and community-based organizations.
- **National Suicide Prevention Life Line** – 1-800-273-8255 for English or 1-888-628-9454 for Spanish
- **National Domestic Violence Hotline** – 1-800-799-7233 and TTY 1-800-787-3224
- **Veteran's Crisis Line** – 1-800-273-TALK (8255)
- **The Eldercare Locator** – 1-800-677-1116 – Resources for Senior Citizens

- **The Disaster Distress Helpline, 1-800-985-5990,** provides immediate crisis counseling to people affected by the coronavirus pandemic
- **Centers for Disease Control and Prevention** (CDC) cdc.gov

HELPFUL SCRIPTURES TO MEDITATE ON DURING THIS DIFFICULT TIME

Psalm 119:105 says, "Your word is a lamp to my feet and a light for my path"

When needing COURAGE: Psalm 138:3; Ephesians 6:10-13

When facing DANGER: Psalm 91:1-16; Psalm 121:1-8

When you have DOUBTS about your salvation: John 3:16; 1 John 5:11-13

When needing help in God's ability to be FAITHFUL: 1 Peter 1:5; Philippians 1:6

When in FINANCIAL need: Psalm 34:10; Philippians 4:19

When needing FORGIVENESS: Hebrews 4:15-16; 1 John 1:9

When seeking GUIDANCE: Proverbs 3:5-6; James 1:5

When LONELY and DEPRESSED: Psalm 23:1-6; Hebrews 13:5

When facing PAIN: Matthew 11:28

When your PATIENCE is being tried: Romans 8:28-29; James 1:2-4

When seeking PEACE in a stressful time: John 14:27, 16:33; Philippians 4:6-7

When filled with sinful PRIDE: 1 Corinthians 4:7; Philippians 2:3-8

When burdened with many PROBLEMS: 1 Peter 5:7; Psalm 55:22

When needing REST: Matthew 11:28-30; Galatians 6:9

When driven by SELFISH DESIRE: Philippians 4:8; 1 John 2:15-17

When facing SORROW: 2 Corinthians 1:3-5; Romans 8:26-28

When SUFFERING: 2 Corinthians 4:17; Psalm 34:19

When facing TEMPTATION: 1 Corinthians 10:13; James 1:2-4, 12-15

When being treated UNFAIRLY: 1 Peter 4:12-15; 1 Peter 2:19-23

When feeling WEAK and INADEQUATE: 2 Corinthians 12:9-10; Philippians 4:13

When needing to over FEAR: Mark 5:36, Isiah 41:10

When need for HEALING BROKEN HEART: Psalm 147:3, Psalm 34:18, Isaiah 61:1-3

When facing REJECTION: Isaiah 43:18-19

When in need of HEALING: Isaiah 53:5, Jeremiah 30:7, Exodus 15:26

QUESTIONS AND THOUGHTS TO PONDER

HOW DO I START?

WHERE DO I START?

HOW CAN I SEE MYSELF STRONG?

HOW DO I ADAPT?

HOW DID I OVERCOME THIS?

HOW HAS THIS HELPED ME GROW?

WHAT CAN I LEARN FROM THIS EXPERIENCE?

WILL I APPRECIATE MY LOVED ONES AS A GIFT?

PRACTICE BEING FULLY PRESENT

DON'T TAKE LIFE FOR GRANTED

ABOUT THE AUTHOR

Nita Reevon is a compassionate Registered Nurse with over 30 years of experience, working in various areas of nursing to include critical care and emergency rooms across the country as a travel nurse. Nursing has been her primary ministry for helping others. She knows first-hand that life is full of challenges and that every moment is an opportunity to practice faith by seeking the good in every situation. She shares some of her life experiences of overcoming obstacles in her own life and tells how she used those obstacles as a stepping stone to rise above her circumstances.

She graduated with her Master's Degree in Business Administration and Healthcare Management from the University of Phoenix. Her book, "From Grief to Strength" is her first published work as an Author. Her easy-to-read style of writing makes understanding God's Word digestible for nearly anyone in need of a comforting Word.

Printed in the United States
by Baker & Taylor Publisher Services